# Gay Male
# Christian Couples

*Life Stories*

**ANDREW K. T. YIP**

PRAEGER

**Westport, Connecticut
London**

**Library of Congress Cataloging-in-Publication Data**

Yip, Andrew K. T., 1963–
    Gay male Christian couples : life stories / Andrew K. T. Yip.
      p.    cm.
    Includes bibliographical references and index.
    ISBN 0–275–95730–6 (alk. paper)
    1. Gay male couples—Great Britain—Social conditions.  2. Gay
male couples—Religious life—Great Britain.  3. Christian gays—
Great Britain—Social conditions.  4. Homosexuality—Great Britain—
Religious aspects—Christianity.  I. Title.
    HQ76.2.G7Y56  1997
    306.76′62′0941—dc21      96–37694

British Library Cataloguing in Publication Data is available.

Library of Congress Catalog Card Number: 96–37694
ISBN: 0–275–95730–6

First published in 1997

Praeger Publishers, 88 Post Road West, Westport, CT 06881
An imprint of Greenwood Publishing Group, Inc.

Printed in the United States of America

The paper used in this book complies with the
Permanent Paper Standard issued by the National
Information Standards Organization (Z39.48–1984).

10 9 8 7 6 5 4 3 2 1

**Copyright Acknowledgments**

The author and publisher gratefully acknowledge permission to reprint
portions of the following articles:

Andrew K. T. Yip. 1996. Gay Christian Couples and Blessing Ceremonies.
*Theology & Sexuality* 4: 100–117. Sheffield Academic Press, used with
permission.

Andrew K. T. Yip. 1996. Gay Christians and Their Participation in the
Gay Subculture. *Deviant Behavior* 17: 297–318. Taylor & Francis, 1996,
used with permission.

Andrew K. T. Yip. 1997. Attacking the Attacker: Gay Christians Talk Back.
*British Journal of Sociology* 48, 1:113–127. London School of Economics,
used with permission.

This book is dedicated to my mother who, in her own quiet ways, taught me to appreciate the beauty of simplicity.

# Contents

# Tables

# Acknowledgements

Conducting this study and writing this book have been a very important and meaningful chapter of my life. Many people have made significant contributions to it in a myriad of ways. Prof. Nigel Fielding and Dr. Alan Clarke provided me with the most professional guidance I could ever expect during the study. I am particularly indebted to Prof. Fielding for his advice on the book. I have also received valuable assistance from many individuals along the way. Among them are: Richard Cunliffe, Richard Kirker, Niall Johnston, Malcolm Johnson, Ford Hickson and Prof. Tony Coxon of Project SIGMA.

My family members, particularly Margaret and Sam, have given me much support and courage over the years, for which I am eternally grateful. I also thank my dear friends who have given me so much strength to carry on these past few years. Elspeth, Mabel, Phang Phang, Chooi Khum, Derek, Joan, Yasmin and Nena & Thanos, thank you!

I am also grateful for the assistance provided by Alan Sturmer of Greenwood Press and Elise Oranges, my copyeditor. Catherine Lyons, my production editor, has been most encouraging and professional, which makes the collaboration a very positive experience.

My respondents, the unsung heroes of this book, have made the study and the book possible. I am deeply touched by their willingness in sharing with me their experiences. I have learned a lot. I thank them from the bottom of my heart.

Finally, Noel Jones, my partner, has always been there for me. Thank you for sharing this adventure with me.

# Introduction

Having been informed by her extraordinary perceptiveness, despite my conscientious pretense, that I was in a partnership with a man she had met only once, my sister wrote to me on 24 March 1994:

> Well, I can see that your relationship with Noel is not just an ordinary one. Both of you are not only friends. When I saw the both of you, I understood. Now, I am not being a busy-body. I am not making any comments. I am just worried about you. I don't have much knowledge about homosexuality. If you feel you would like to talk to me about it, I am always here. I think I have written enough. I only pray to God that I have done the right thing in writing you this letter. I shall now pray and ask the Lord to bring me the best outcome.

Having read my reply to her letter, in which I confirmed her perceptiveness by telling her an aspect of my life that she had never known despite our exceptional closeness, my sister wrote again on 20 April 1994:

> I read your letter quickly once and slowly the second time. I shouldn't have gone swimming, but I did. Before I realized it, I was crying while driving and I couldn't see the road very well. I had to get to the car park quickly, and then I had to let it all out. I cried in the car. I must have cried for 5 to 10 minutes. I didn't cry because of what you told me about what you are. I cried because I now realized that you had gone

through all this alone. Oh God! It must have been horrible for you. I don't blame you for not telling me. I may not be able to understand. I, just like so many people, have had a distorted picture of gays, like their being "sissy" or perhaps being sick or abnormal. In any case, I want to tell you that I fully accept you as you are. You are my brother, a very dear human to me and I love you: gay or not gay. You and your friends, gay or not gay, are always welcome to my home. Are you happy living your life? I suppose it must be tough to live the way you describe, not showing in public. I am here if you want to talk about yourself. The important point is I hope you are happy now.

I write this book primarily for readers typified by my sister. In both her letters, she asked many questions pertaining to homosexuality and same-sex relationships. This book is written for individuals like her who, first and foremost, have the humility to acknowledge their ignorance about this subject and, subsequently, the courage to learn about it despite the possibility of having their long-held perceptions seriously challenged. These are brave people.

Homosexuality per se is still a very unfamiliar subject for a lot of people, let alone same-sex partnerships. When I began, late in 1992, the research on which this book is broadly based, two male acquaintances of mine commented that they could not see a justifiable cause for such an effort. They maintained that while they could understand how two men could end up having sex due to lust or perversion, they found it inconceivable that two men were capable of being in love and wanting to establish a committed partnership. Another female friend commented, "So you are interested in finding out who is the 'husband' and who is the 'wife,' and who is the leader and who is the follower?"

Many people, like my sister, are asking a host of questions about same-sex partnerships (I shall henceforth focus on gay male partnerships, since this is the subject matter of this book. The social circumstances under which lesbian partnerships are formed and develop warrant a separate treatment.) How do two men fall in love? How do they manage their domestic life? Do they fight over who is to do the washing-up? Do they share everything from underwear to money? What do they do in bed? How do they organize their relationships with the outside world? I hope this book will succeed in answering some of these questions.

Of course, not everyone wants to learn about this seemingly disturbing issue. To learn is to be humbled, and some people are not capable of that. They would prefer to shield themselves from this subject out of fear, prejudice, and contempt. In June 1995, I attended a workshop on Christianity and homosexuality in which almost all of the participants were heterosexuals committed to "helping" gay Christians. One male participant who learned about my research asked me what I thought about gay male Christian couples on the whole. I said, "Well, they are very courageous really, hanging on to their partnerships despite the lack of support from the Church." With apparent displeasure, he answered, "Oh well, I still think they are perverts!" Many people, like this man, have decapacitated their ability to learn as a result of their arrogant sense of moral superiority and self-righteousness. Scott Peck calls these fundamentalist Bible believers "inerrantists," who "believe that the Bible is not only the divinely inspired word of God but the actual transcribed, unaltered word of God, and that it is subject to only *one* kind of literal interpretation, namely *theirs*. Such thinking, to my mind, only impoverishes the Bible." [1] [Italics added]

In August 1995, I wrote to the editor of a national newspaper in response to its reporting that a gay male Christian in partnership was denied the opportunity by his parish church to be the godparent of his nephew despite the full support of the child's parents. In the edited letter, I mentioned that my research reveals that gay male Christians are capable of forming committed and long-standing partnerships. [2] I further argued that, in this particular case, the man's ability and character, not his sexuality, should be the determining factor in the evaluation of his suitability to be a godparent. [3] I received some positive responses to my letter. However, I also received a note from an anonymous (naturally) person with the stern message, "Fuck you, jerk!" I think this message needs no elaboration.

In April 1996, I attended an academic conference to present a paper on how gay male Christians manage their stigma. During a coffee break, I was having a conversation with an eminent sociologist. He asked me what my research was about, and I said, "Gay Christians." He immediately replied, "I don't like gay Christians!" Amused and not wanting to let him off the hook easily, I asked with pretended innocence, "Oh, tell me why!" He sternly answered, "Because I am a Roman Catholic, you know!" He then walked away. The next day, I was scheduled as the second speaker in the session. This sociologist was there for the first and third presentations, but stayed away during mine. It appears that Voltaire's famous dictum, "I disapprove of what you say, but I will defend to death your right to say it" is easier said than done, even for a knowledgeable academic! I have often found it sociologically fascinating to encounter academics who are extraordinarily knowledgeable yet lamentably narrowminded.

I also write this book for gay men who are considering the prospect of establishing a partnership and those who are already in one. This book is not designed to be a self-help manual specifically. Readers will need to look elsewhere for this. [4] Nevertheless, it is not a demanding task to identify the lessons that we can learn from the gay male partnerships reported in this book. I hope that this book will sufficiently inform readers in this category about the costs and rewards of being in a gay male partnership. I do not propose a blueprint for an "ideal" gay male partnership, because an "ideal" gay male partnership does not exist. A partnership is a relational process. Each partner brings to it his strengths and shortcomings. What makes a successful partnership is the partners' ability and willingness to effectively negotiate and constantly define the parameters of the partnership whenever the need arises. A partnership is an individualized process, the management of which should be contingent upon the partners themselves, not on an externally imposed "ideal."

It is clear by now that this book does not aim to address a specialized sociological audience. Readers interested in more academic materials should refer to my other writings.[5] I have also included in the Bibliography many relevant academic references. Nevertheless, it is not difficult to tease out the primary sociological theme embedded in this book: the organization of intimate relationships in postmodern society. In this case, the focus is on gay male Christians, an underresearched sexual and religious minority. Their experiences undoubtedly would contribute to the sociological discourse on intimate relationship that currently is based almost entirely on the experiences of heterosexuals. There is a need for the boundary of this discourse to be extended.

I adopt a "story-telling" approach in the writing of this book. This book contains the stories of 68 gay male couples who kindly allowed me to enter into the private sphere of their partnerships. These are their stories, their lived experiences, from which we can learn about human nature and social relationships. We can view this book as a document of their love. Whether we are comfortable with this love is a different matter. We need to search our conscience about that.

The management of a partnership as an intimate relationship is a balancing act. Joseph De Cecco argues that a gay partnership consists of "the intricate balancing of the obligations of reciprocity and the aspirations for change." [6] The partners constantly strive to balance the position of their partnership on this spectrum. If the balance tilts toward the direction of the obligation end, the partnership faces the possibility of being excessively rigid and stultifying. On the other hand, if the partnership tips toward the aspiration end, it would end up being precarious and amorphous.

Inasmuch as a partnership is embedded within a social web, it is important to also consider how both partners relate to the outside world as individuals and as a social unit. The internal and external dimensions are inexplicably intertwined.[7] Both partners have to learn to cope with the challenges in both dimensions. Thus, no stories about a partnership would be complete if either of the dimensions is missing.

I focus on the internal dimension of these partnerships in the first half of this book. I set the scene by presenting issues pertaining to the beginning period of these partnerships. I then discuss the various domestic arrangements of the partnerships and the ways in which these couples manage conflicts. Finally, I examine the different styles the couples have developed in managing their finances.

Beginning with Chapter 5, I gradually extend the parameter of the stories to the external dimension of the partnerships. Having discussed the couples' own sex lives, I address the sensitive issue of sexual exclusivity. This issue has the potential to destabilize a partnership. How do couples facing this issue manage it? Also, since the majority of the couples attend local churches, how do they manage the potential difficulty with their fellow parishioners and clergy? The stories continue with a look at the couples' participation in the gay subculture, a milieu where they are, in principle, fully accepted as they are.

A brief note about the respondents. The 68 gay male Christian couples were primarily recruited through gay Christian organizations in Britain. Each respondent completed a postal questionnaire. I later interviewed a subsample of 30 couples. I have changed all of the respondents' names in order to protect their identity. More details about the respondents and research methods can be found in the Appendix.

In the meantime, let me retreat to the background. Let the stories unfold. Let's listen and learn!

# CHAPTER 1

# The Beginning Period

Given that gay male couples constitute a largely hidden segment of our society, we have very little knowledge about the factors affecting the initiation of these partnerships. This chapter presents the histories of these partnerships. It attempts to answer several questions: Where and how did the couples meet? Is similarity between partners in religious beliefs a primary selection criterion? Was sex featured prominently in their first encounter? Given that they carry no cultural baggage about relationship formation, did the couples begin with explicit agreements about the parameters of their partnerships? How do they, as partners, refer to each other? Have they solemnized their partnerships in blessing ceremonies?

## THE FIRST ENCOUNTER

Alan Bell and Martin Weinberg comment that the lack of social acceptance offers gay men little opportunity to meet in safe environments other than the "sexual marketplaces" that the commercial gay scene provides.[1] However, the experiences of the interviewed couples reveal that they met in a wide range of social settings. The majority of the couples I interviewed met in nonreligious social settings such as educational institutions, the workplace, and social gatherings organized by friends. George and Richard, a noncohabiting couple of 8 years who first met at their workplace, walk down memory lane:

*George*: We used to work together in the same building. Richard used to be this person on the 8th floor who was never there because he was out working. When he was there, he wasn't working, he just looked out and smiled with a little twinkling in his eyes.

*Richard*: And then we started. I think George went down to the second floor and I was at the second floor. We just started to talk to one another and there were a couple of other people whom George was friendly with and I was friendly with. So we started going out for drinks and then we started playing Trivial Pursuit at the office as a foursome and so on. And then I asked him to come to a couple of things in my home and then he stayed the night. Certainly the development of partnership was initiated by me because I then invited him to stay in my home and invited him to different things in the church, and so on. So the development was initiated by me.

Not surprisingly, some couples first met in a religious setting such as a gay Christian group or the church. With some assistance from mutual friends, the ground for the establishment of a relationship was laid. Keith, a medical professional, met his partner Jerry, a teacher, with an extra push from a friend. They have been together for 13 years now.

*Keith*: I was convenor of [a Lesbian and Gay Christian Movement (LGCM) local group] and I got a letter from a young man asking about this group which was meeting in [city]. That was Jerry. So I replied to his letter and told him when and where the meetings were. He turned up one day, and we were introduced to each other by James.

*Jerry*: I fancied Keith very much when I saw him at the meeting. James picked that up and then made sure that we got to chat to each other and dance together in the disco later.

James, an administrator in his late 30s, met Nigel who is 13 years his junior at church. They have been together for 13 years and 3 months. They tell their story below:

*James*: I saw Nigel at the church with a friend of mine called Jennifer. It was at quite an early stage of my coming out. I told myself that I would like to meet this good-looking young man. So I made a point to meet Jennifer. In fact, she had already decided that she wanted Nigel to meet me because she knew me as quite a mature Christian. He was a new Christian. She thought I would be a good influence on him. How wrong she was! And we just met and we hit it off really quickly at the back of the church. I happened to ask him if he was interested in playing squash and he said he was a squash player. It wasn't true, but he said he was. That must have said something about him! So that was how we met. The rest of the story is really a growing friendship, and in the course of that friendship we came to understand more about our respective sexualities. It was a natural progression.

*Nigel*: So that was the story of our growing and developing. Gradually we became close and intimate. And the intimacy developed as the relationship became closer. So the squash game was our first date. I had never played squash before in my life!

*James*: So we met for squash and we went for a meal afterwards. But it was all very tentative. If Nigel had been an out and "together" [well-integrated] gay person I am sure I would have responded very quickly to that. But Nigel was at the beginning of coming to terms with it [his sexuality] and I was in the process of it. Obviously the relationship was very tentative and in many ways very exploratory.

*Nigel*: As we got to know each other better I realized how strong the feelings we had developed were. We created something that had a very strong bond.

Given the proliferation of the gay press, telephone chatlines, and dating agencies, it is not surprising to note that some respondents met their partners through these channels. Rick, a priest in his late 30s and Walter, a financial professional also in his late 30s, are in a 3-year-old partnership. They met through a gay dating agency. They tell their story:

*Rick*: We met through Gay Link International [a gay dating agency]. We made an appointment and met in front of the Planetarium. It was the night that the 01 became 071 and 081 [London area telephone codes]. There were laser lights being flashed around the Post Office Tower. It was quite dramatic.

*Walter*: I thought it was rather nice. It was a blind date. We went for a drink and we went to find something to eat. And then we came back to my place and had coffee and we ended

up having sex. I liked Rick and said that I wanted to see him
again. He was enthusiastic. So it started from there.

Ryan and Nick, a relatively young couple, have been together for only
one year. They also met through an advertisement in a gay weekly:

> *Ryan*: We met through a lonely heart advert [personal adver-
> tisement] in *Capital Gay*. Nick responded to me. I had writ-
> ten in *Capital Gay* an advert which was... I couldn't remem-
> ber it [the content].

> *Nick*: Thirty-five, professional, intelligent, cuddly, interested
> in theatre, music, films, seeks new friends. I remember it
> wasn't a very original one.

> *Ryan*: We then spoke on the phone first of all. Then we ar-
> ranged to meet. We went to [cafe's name] and we went to see
> a movie. So we had a glass of wine, a coffee, and chatted
> away and watched the film. And then we went for a drink in
> a pub. And then we stood outside [name] tube station and
> chatted away. We said we would like to meet up again. And
> he went back home.

Some couples actually met in the commercial gay scene. Simon
and John, who have been in partnership for 14 years, met in a gay
club. They recount:

> *Simon*: Well, I had seen this young man [John] before in a lit-
> tle [gay] drinking club that I used to go to after work when
> the theatre finished. I always thought he was very smart. He
> was always in black and white, impeccably dressed, and he
> has a beautiful bum. He came up to me one day when I was
> very very drunk, and he said, "Has anyone ever told you that
> you look like Colin Davis?" And I said, "What's wrong with
> mediocrity?"

> *John*: And so I knew that he was obviously very intelligent,
> because most people told me that Colin Davis was a big star.
> Very few people knew how ordinary he was! I couldn't think
> of anything else to say. And then I came up to him a couple of
> days later and I said, "Is it safe to talk to you now?" And we
> chatted for a while. I suppose the romantic part is that we
> wined and dined each other for weeks and weeks. Six weeks!

Similarly, Neil and Damien, both social workers, who have been together for 14 years and 3 months, also met in a gay pub. They poked fun at each other as I listened to their partnership history.

*Neil*: It was Sunday 11 February 1979, and I'd been a week or so out of what wasn't really a relationship, but it's what I had at that time. [A friend] had a very bad time. He had split up with his boyfriend. We both needed cheering up. So we went to this pub where we knew mutual people. It must have been about 9.30 p. m. and the pub began to get packed. Damien came into the pub, I wasn't aware of him to begin with because our group was the largest group in there. It was quite noisy, but it was a friendly group. One or two people in the group must have asked him to join us, which he did. I eventually became aware of him. I suppose he came and sat next to me.

*Damien*: No! You came rushing over to me and said you would like a drink!

*Neil*: He always maintains that I came up to him and said, "Would you like a drink?" But I honestly can't remember that. He always makes it sound as if I ran all over him! But I don't know what really happened. We just started talking. We stayed there and chatted for a while and people saying "Good night" and left us there.

*Damien*: I gave you a lift home and we stood chatting at the gate for a while. I said, "I'm off tomorrow, can I see you?" You said, "I'm not working at the moment." And we met the next day. Here we are today. It just went on!

### How Important Is the Partner's Religion?

Almost two-thirds of the respondents I interviewed do not consider their partners' religion a main selection criterion for the establishment of their partnerships. Neil, whom I have just mentioned, is a Roman Catholic in his late 30s. He asserts:

No. When I first came to know Damien [his partner], I didn't know what his religion was, although we met through a religious group. I was part of the group; he was not. He just happened to come where the group was meeting. He came into the social side of it. I had no idea what his religion was to begin with. I don't think I was bothered. It was later that I

found out what his religion was. Already at that stage I
wanted to pursue the relationship, so that wasn't going to be
a problem.

Neil's experience is shared by many, like Rick, a Church of England priest in his late 30s who met his partner Walter through the
Gay Link International. I have told the story about their first meeting. Rick did not consider Walter's religion important when he decided to pursue a relationship with him. He recalls:

Well, I mean there was no concern at all. In fact, when we
first met, as far as I was aware, he wasn't religious. He
didn't really have much religion. He had a religious background at school. But he sort of rejected most of it. Then
eventually he sort of came round to be a practicing Anglican.
But certainly it wasn't anything to do with me requiring it. I
suppose once or twice I said that it would be nice if he came
round and listened to me preach so that I could get some
feedback.

At present, Walter is a confirmed Anglican. He attends Rick's
church on a weekly basis and in general enjoys the experience. Nigel,
an engineering professional in his early 20s, is affiliated to the
Church of England. He speaks in resonance with Neil's view:

I supposed I was glad that he was a Christian person. He be-
longed to the Salvation Army. In some way, I regarded that
as a rather peculiar sort of religion. It was certainly not for
me. But I don't think it would have made an enormous difference whether he was Christian or not.

These accounts are not unexpected. Given the scarcity of accepting and conducive environments for gay men to meet and foster relationships, they are only too glad when a potential partner comes
along. That person's religion is therefore not a main concern, as they
are cognizant of the fact that being inflexible in this respect would
further limit their opportunity to meet a potential partner.

Although religion is not a specifically important criterion in partner selection, the similarity of religious beliefs can provide a fertile
ground for the seed of love to germinate and grow. Some couples met
in religious settings such as the church. I have already introduced
James and Nigel, who met in such a context. James acknowledges
that religion did facilitate the initiation of his partnership with Nigel.

I suppose it's true to say that the relationship arose in many
ways out of mutual belief and respect for spirituality, and it

has developed so much along those lines, and it's difficult to imagine anything other than that. One of the strongest things that attracted me to Nigel is his respect for, and involvement in, his own spirituality. So I suppose if that were not there, there would have been a major doubt. It may have worked in other ways though, but it may not.

Morgan and James, both retired, met way back in the late 1940s. James, then an undergraduate, came to know about Morgan at the college chapel, where Morgan was the chaplain. Religion has played a significant, though not exclusive, role in the initiation of their partnership. They tell their story below:

*Morgan*: Well that [James' religious beliefs] certainly helped. It was something that we had in common up to a point. When I first knew James he was a Presbyterian and I was from the high church Anglican and still am. He has since been confirmed in the Church of England. Yes, that certainly helped, yes. I don't think it was a decisive factor in our coming together, but it certainly was of importance in the relationship.

*James*: It was a great help that he had been the chaplain. After all, it was he who brought me into the Anglican Church because when we met I was still a Presbyterian because I had been brought up that way. So he was in that relationship of guiding my religion at that stage.

Nevertheless, some respondents emphatically mention that similar religious beliefs between partners is of paramount importance as the basis of the partnerships. Robert, a Church of England priest, explains:

I think it is important to me that God is part of the relationship, especially because psychologically speaking there is so much to undermine your security. You have to be very clear that it is a Christian-based thing. It's a Christian vocation. Our love comes from God.

His partner, Michael, also a priest with the Church of England, argues in support of his view:

Yes. My religion is such a key factor to being me. So to actually share my life with somebody with a different persuasion would be very difficult.

Other respondents appear to adopt the principle of compromise if there is a need. While acknowledging the importance of similarity in religious beliefs, some are willing to compromise if their partners are non-Christian, but not dismissive of their own religious beliefs. Calvin, a young priest with the Church of England, has been in a partnership for 5 years. He expresses this point:

> It [not sharing similar religious beliefs] could have been a stumbling block. I couldn't sensibly have a relationship with someone who is strongly opposed to my faith and the direction I was going. So, that wouldn't have worked if there had been someone quite antagonistic towards what I am doing. The only thing that is actually important is that he was willing to be sympathetic towards it even if he didn't want to take on that faith and religion himself... and not defining himself in quite the same way.

It appears that most respondents consider the similarity of religious beliefs not a main concern for the development of their partnerships. As I have mentioned, this is most likely due to their realization about the difficulty of finding a potential partner in their everyday life.

### Sex at First Sight?

Was the first meeting of these couples sexual in nature? Only five interviewed couples, who met through advertisements in gay publications and private parties, fall into this category. The majority of the couples did not have sex during their first meeting. However, more than ten couples engaged in sexual activity in their second meeting, which, on certain occasions, took place on the following day. Their experiences appear to confirm what Letitia Peplau and Susan Cochran report, that 60 percent of the gay male couples they studied had sex for the first time within one month after their first meeting.[2] The dating scripts of gay men are also found to be more sexual than those of heterosexuals and lesbians.[3] The following comment explains why sex features largely:

> The whole thing started as a sexual act, then led on to a relationship. So I think in this case it worked from sex in the beginning. If you get it right, it is a very good crude basis for it because if they like each other then they won't have many problems in other areas. (Paul, an actor in his mid-50s)

This comment resonates with the experiences of many couples I interviewed. Casual and anonymous sex, being highly available in gay social settings, often is used as a yardstick to gauge the viability and potential for the development of a relationship. Inter-partner sexual compatibility is viewed as a good basis for the development of a relationship.

However, for some couples, both partners deliberately refrained from any sexual activity until they were certain about their mutual commitment to the partnership. This is the scenario for Simon and John, who took six weeks of deliberation before engaging in any form of sexual activity, although they met each other frequently during that "courtship" period. Their past experiences inform them that the relationship they have established has the potential to evolve into a committed partnership. Sex was therefore withheld in order to avoid premature emotional involvement. In this connection, Simon, an administrator in his mid-30s, relates, "I know the importance of this potential relationship. I didn't want to rush things." John, a musician in his late 30s, gives a similar response, "I think I had made a conscious decision not to do anything because I wanted to see what he was like first."

It appears that the couples I interviewed hold different views as to how largely sex was featured in the beginning of their partnerships. However, the majority engaged in sexual activity during either the first or second meeting, with the typical intention of using sex to assess their compatibility with each other. This, argued Martin Weinberg and Colin William, is typical of the majority of gay encounters.[4]


## EXPLICIT AGREEMENT

Not having any normative framework within which a partnership can be constructed, most gay couples have to engage in the formation of the framework itself. This compels them to undergo what Anthony Giddens calls "effort bargaining," an ongoing process of negotiation between partners to ensure that the constitutional arrangement they make generates mutual satisfaction and fulfilment.[5] Does this mean that the partners explicitly negotiate the parameters of the partnership in the beginning period?

Few couples I interviewed explicitly drew the parameters of their partnerships when they started. Those who did report that the nature of their explicit agreements has been constantly modified as the partnerships progress. This is certainly the case for Richard and George, a noncohabiting couple who have been together for 8 years. Although they started with an explicit agreement that their partnership should be sexually exclusive, they decided two years later that the partnership should adopt sexual nonexclusivity. The change of this constitutional arrangement proved problematic and almost led to the dissolution of their partnership. They subsequently decided to return to sexual exclusivity to restore the stability of their partnership. I will tell their story in greater detail in Chapter 5. Suffice it to say at this point that gay partnerships are characterized by a process of constant negotiation, precipitated by the lack of any role models and behavioral blueprint.

The ability they demonstrate in constantly structuring their partnerships depending on circumstantial expediency convincingly challenges the conservative clinical standpoint which is sceptical of the longevity of gay partnerships due to the perceived psychopathological nature of homosexuality. I would argue that it is their *ability* to constantly engage in the process of constant negotiation that makes their partnerships meaningful and workable. The eventual arrangement is therefore less important, since it can be renegotiated as the partnership progresses.

On the whole, the majority of the couples did not, in the beginning, make an explicit agreement about the nature of their partnership. Most couples prefer to adopt a wait-and-see approach, being fully cognizant of the odds against the longevity of a gay partnership. What constitutes the partnership is a process of constant negotiation. Ryan, who has been in a partnership for one year, argues:

> To have an explicit agreement is very clinical. It seems to impose a kind of marriage contract on the relationship. It is just one of those things that just evolves and naturally comes to various conclusions.

This typical response reveals that many couples acknowledge the need to constantly negotiate their expectations of the partnership. The constitutional structure of the partnership therefore has the potential to modify as the partnership progresses. Many couples therefore prefer not to engage in undue negotiation at the beginning of the partnership and prefer to allow the negotiation process to take place as the partnership develops. An appropriate metaphor is provided by Alan, a medical professional in his late 40s, who has been in a cohabiting partnership for 21 years:

> If you are growing a plant, it is no good pulling it up to see how the roots are growing. If you keep pulling it up and looking at the roots, then nothing will ever grow. You have to leave it. Don't inspect it too often, then it will grow quite nicely. If you keep inspecting it and looking at the details, then it will never grow. I don't like discussing things in detail. I like things just to get on and go.

We can see that most gay couples do not consider having an explicit agreement at the beginning of the partnership essential. This is precipitated by their recognition of the in-built odds that work against the longevity of a gay partnership owing to the lack of social support. However, this also conversely gives them the flexibility to negotiate as the partnership develops. This theme will be developed in the subsequent chapters.

## TERM OF REFERENCE

More than 60 percent of the entire sample prefer to use the term *partner* when they refer to their own partners. Most reject other terms such as *lover* or *boyfriend*.[6] To them, *partner* suggests their commitment to each other and equality in a partnership, which the other two terms do not. Rick, a Church of England priest in a 3-year-old partnership, argues:

I think *partner* is probably more honest. The relationship is a partnership, two people working together. I think it implies that there is a sort of dynamic, something we work on together.

Richard, who has been in a partnership for 8 years, argues in the same vein:

*Partner* sounds more like a long-term commitment and therefore I would like to think of us as being in a partnership where we are together and we are equal. So *partner* sounds much more appropriate to me.

The following respondents further outline their rejection of other terms because of their inaccuracy in describing their partnerships:

All other terms I think have different sorts of overtones and also don't accurately imply the nature of our relationship. *Boyfriend* I think indicates something fairly transitory and also a relationship where you see each other occasionally, normally when you are living in different homes and you see each other to go to the movies or to go to social events. *Lover* I think sometimes has connotations of being purely a sexual and physical relationship and not an emotional relationship as well. You talk about a lover in a straight relationship and it often implies quite a bit on the side rather than a monogamous committed relationship. So *partner* these days tends to be the accepted social term for the person you live with, the person who shares your life and it is a useful term as well. (Ryan, administrator, mid-30s)

I suppose *partner* is a good term because it is a descriptive term, but it is also a nonsexual term. It is a term which two people can describe themselves without using heterosexual terminology. There are a lot of other words like *lover*. But I think the word *lover* has a pejorative sense. The term *partner* is a good description because it describes that we are in partnership. We are equal partners. The term suggests equality, where I think for heterosexuality sometimes it can imply a predominance of one over the other. (Michael, priest, early 40s)

It is interesting to note that the respondents' choice of the term *partner* is primarily based on its implications: commitment and equality. This reflects the importance they place on these elements in their partnerships. The term *partner* also is preferred because it does not suggest gender as, for instance, *boyfriend* would. This term is therefore used as a strategy to control information about their sexuality and partnership. Nigel, an engineer in his early 20s, illustrates the need to use this term in his workplace:

*Partner* is a neutral term. For example, at work I can say that I have a partner. That doesn't necessarily bring up the issue of homosexuality because straight people have partners as well. You know, I say, "I have to consult my partner." I think they know my partner is a man. I don't do it intentionally to deceive them. But it is done so that when I make a point, because I think it is important that they know I have somebody else to consider. But I don't necessarily have to bring up the issue of homosexuality. To me, the sex of my partner is irrelevant to the issue.

In the same vein, Kieran, a manager in his late 30s, uses this term to conceal his 18-year-old partnership in certain contexts:

I think *partner* represents a degree of stability and a degree of commitment. It is also a kind of expression you can use within straight company when you want to perhaps talk about your relationship but don't necessarily want to reveal that he is the same sex as yourself. I was very cautious when I went to my current job talking about my partner until I knew that it was safe to some degree to reveal what sex that partner was.

There is a prevalent strong dislike for terms with heavy heterosexual connotations such as *Other Half* and *Spouse*. This is clearly spelt out in the accounts below:

> *Other half* is silly. I am complete. I never like the term. I mean, the Lord in the sense of a marriage union says we become one. We are not two halves. We become one. We are each whole in our own way. So I wouldn't use that term. (James, architect, late 40s)

> *Spouse* is so related to marriage. Of course I do not believe that gay partnerships like mine are on the same level ideally speaking as Christian matrimony. I think the trouble has been that the very great goodness and importance of Christianity matrimony has tended to overshadow or obscure the great goodness to be found in other relationships. (Samuel, retired, mid-60s)

> *Partner* seems to be the most appropriate word because I look at our relationship more as a partnership, because we do things for each other, with each other, to each other, and they are meaningful things. So we are in partnership. I certainly don't want to attach traditional heterosexual labels to it like *husband* or *other half* and what not, because they just really don't seem appropriate. (James, administrator, late 30s)

We can see that even in this area of term of reference that most take for granted, gay men's choices of the appropriate terms reflect both the ideology of equality and the rejection of heterosexual terms. This clearly illustrates their intention to not be subject to heterosexism. Heterosexual relationships in general still are characterized by the dominant-subordinate model that many of them assiduously attempt to jettison.

## BLESSING CEREMONIES

Recent years have seen the debate, in both the secular and religious contexts, of the issue of legal recognition of same-sex partnerships. Many gay people argue that this legal recognition will precipitate a greater degree of acceptance of homosexuality in society at large. In addition, recognizing same-sex partnerships is an extension of gay people's human rights to their love. The British government is urged to follow the footsteps of its fellow European counterparts, namely, the Netherlands, Sweden, Norway, Iceland, Greenland, and

Denmark, which have various forms of legal recognition for same-sex partnerships. In the United States, the State of Hawaii was ordered in December 1996 by the Supreme Court to issue marriage licenses to same-sex couples. Although the case is now suspended pending an appeal by the island's government, many gay people consider this a landmark achievement.

On the other hand, some gay people are concerned about the energy and resources of the gay community being spent on this issue. They are of the opinion that these resources can be used more effectively in areas that affect all gay people, partnered or otherwise. They assert that issues such as HIV/AIDS and the discrimination currently suffered by lesbians and gay men in employment, the armed forces, and other aspects of everyday life deserve greater attention.

Inasmuch as legal recognition is still not possible in Britain, I was inclined to find out if the couples have had blessing ceremonies of any kind to solemnize their partnerships. I attempted to find out why some are supportive of the idea of having their partnerships solemnized while some find the idea repugnant.

None of the couples reported that they had had blessing ceremonies. Only one couple had had a symbolic ceremony initiated by the couple themselves. Calvin, a Church of England priest, and Clive, a financial professional, categorically reject the idea of having the blessing ceremony conducted in a church because of its intolerant attitude towards gay Christians:

> *Calvin*: We don't want a church blessing because the church doesn't bless us. What is the point of doing it in the church that condemns us, to pretend in a blessing? We went out to somewhere that was special to us where there would be nobody else around. We planned it for months. We wrote some prayers before that happened, and we wrote vows. We exchanged vows and we exchanged gifts.

> *Clive*: It was one event that put everything in a concrete form. It summarized everything. It wasn't about blessing [by the Church]. It was about vows. And also it was a symbol of commitment.

In spite of the lack of support and recognition from the Church and society at large, Calvin and Clive proceeded with a ceremony of their own to solemnize their partnership. This personalized ceremony, as they have argued, is a symbol of their mutual commitment and love.

Many couples who have not yet had a blessing ceremony of any kind are supportive of the idea for two primary reasons. First, a blessing ceremony is a public celebration of their mutual commitment and the expression of gratitude to supportive individuals. Second, it is a political statement about the existence of gay couples and their ability in establishing committed relationships. Nigel, an engineering professional, and James, an administrator, who have been in a co-habiting partnership for 3 years and 3 months, strongly express the first view:

> *Nigel*: To have a ceremony is to principally say thank you to our parents, family, and friends for supporting us and for enabling us to establish what we have got. That's the main reason. To thank God. I suppose subsidiarily, to say to the world that we are serious with what we have got.

> *James*: [The ceremony] as a blessing, yes. But more as a cele-bration and a thank-you, probably to be held in the church. But I haven't closed my mind about using other places or a country which is special to us. It would be as meaningful as the church. Also I think as humans we have a need for ritual. It's something very deep and bonding about having appropri-ate rituals. I feel that that will be important. I don't want a marriage service. I don't want to pretend a family relation-ship. I want to feel that whenever there is a ritual, we can find and develop and equip our lives together.

Paul, a civil servant, and Kieran, an accountant, express a similar view for their desire to have a blessing ceremony in the future:

> *Paul*: It did cross my mind that where there are formal cere-monies or properly conducted ceremonies with an established liturgy, [blessing ceremonies] are right. I think it might be better to do it that way. I am quite happy to do it in this country if we are able to do it. I think it is sort of a public ex-pression of commitment. I think it is just a nice thing to pro-fess our feelings.

> *Kieran*: It is the celebration of our feelings. I suppose both being Christians, we want to make vows to each other before God. It just finalizes it.

We can see that while they acknowledge the religious or ritualis-tic significance of a blessing ceremony, they are not adamant about using the church exclusively for such an event. They even express the desire to do it overseas in a country such as the Netherlands or Denmark, where there are legal provisions for same-sex partner-ships. They are also emphatic in not wishing the ceremony to be misconstrued as a mimicry of heterosexual marriage. This point of view is prevalent among the interviewed couples. In fact, many couples were dismissive of a blessing ceremony on this ground. I will elaborate on this later.

A blessing ceremony is also perceived as a political statement about the existence of gay couples and a public declaration of their commitment for each other against the stereotype that gay men are not interested in and capable of long-standing relationships. It also demands that the Church and society at large acknowledge and accept their indisputable existence. Richard and George, who have been together for 8 years and attend the same local church, argue the need for recognition in the church. George, in his late 40s, asserts:

> You see I don't have a desire to repeat a marriage ceremony or anything like that. But what I have a desire to do is to have a commitment to each other that is acknowledged by the church. I think quite strongly that because of the life I am now leading, it should therefore be blessed by the church. That would be an open acknowledgement of our commitment to our lifestyle within the church, and repeated by the church for us.

The desire not to mimic a heterosexual marriage in having a blessing ceremony is reiterated in George's view. Going one step further, Samuel, who is in a 27-year-old partnership, argues for recognition of his partnership not just by the Church, but also the government:

> I do think that we ought to have a civil register for gay partnerships in this country, because I feel very strongly that if anything happened to Ricky [his partner], the government would confiscate quite a sizeable chunk of his estate which really ought to come to me. So I feel very militant about this. I think we ought to have equal rights. I think there should be a civil register, but then I think people should choose, if they are religious, to have a blessing if they want.

To Samuel, the legalization of same-sex partnerships is of paramount importance, regardless of whether a couple decides to hold a blessing ceremony or not. His view resonates with the argument that the basic benefits accorded to heterosexual couples such as rights of inheritance and tax relief should be legally extended to same-sex couples. This is an issue of fundamental human rights.[7]

In sum, a blessing ceremony is perceived by those in support of it as primarily an opportunity to thank God, each other, and, if conducted publicly, to thank the supportive individuals around them. Besides being a symbol of commitment, the blessing ceremony also can be a political statement in correcting the long-held but erroneous clinical standpoint that gay men are not capable of establishing meaningful and committed partnerships.

In spite of the desire to have a blessing ceremony, private or public, most couples have not had one. Two major factors are responsible for this scenario: the fear of exposure, and the lack of maturity and readiness of the partnership itself. Michael, whose partner, Cliff, is a Church of England priest, expresses this concern before the decision on the ordination of women priests was taken by the Church of England in 1994:

> It is difficult because of Cliff's profession [as a priest]. Right now the Church [of England] is going through really great changes with women priests coming in. It is such a drastic change that it has made the whole structure very shaky. A lot of people are wary right now of doing anything out of the ordinary because everything is not quite firm.

The need for the concealment of social information about the partnership as a result of concern about negative social repercussions also is expressed by Richard and George, whom I have discussed earlier. In spite of their perception that a blessing ceremony is an important political statement to be made, George asserts that he would only consent to having a ceremony if a suitable and trustworthy priest could be found. He insists that the priest chosen to officiate at the occasion must be a complete stranger to him, whom he can choose not to meet again after the ceremony. This concern appears to be the main factor affecting the decision-making about when and how to conduct the blessing ceremony for many couples.

Some couples are planning a blessing ceremony when the right time comes. Luke and Mark are both civil servants in their mid-30s. They have been together for 8 years and 2 months when I interviewed them. They told me why they would like a blessing ceremony in about two years' time:

> *Luke*: Because [by then] we will have been together ten years. Having seen straight relationships and other gay relationships that haven't lasted and don't last more than two or three years, I'm proud at eight years. Ten years is a nice round figure. It would be nice on our tenth anniversary to a have a blessing ceremony followed by a party at the house.
>
> *Mark*: Well, yes. For the past year or so we have been discussing off and on a tenth year celebration anyway. And the thought of a blessing has come up and yes because we were going to have some sort of celebration anyway, therefore it's a

good opportunity that if we are going to be blessed, why not combine it? We can also demonstrate that we are a partnership and that as a gay couple we are more than just bed partners.

### Rejection of Blessing Ceremonies

At the other end of the spectrum are couples who are dismissive of the idea of having a blessing ceremony for three primary reasons. The first relates closely to their perception that a blessing ceremony mimics a heterosexual marriage. Given that same-sex partnerships differ from those of cross-sex ones, opting for a ceremony that apes the heterosexual model would be inappropriate. Alan, a Church of England priest who has been in a partnership for 10 years and 2 months, argues in this connection:

I find it [blessing ceremony] difficult. It would feel like you are pretending to be married. In a myriad of ways that makes me quite angry because we are not allowed to be legally married. So it would be like pretending that is not right. I have a lot of difficulty with marriage as an institution. I think it is oppressive.

Alan's view is supported by the following arguments:

I think it is rather silly. Homosexual relationships are not really the same as heterosexual relationships. Having a blessing ceremony would be like a marriage or saying that it is like a marriage. (Marcus, a Church of England priest in his mid-30s)

I disapprove of it [a blessing ceremony]. Pretending to be something you are not. You are what you are. You accept what you are. You live in that context. You don't have to pretend. Marriage is for heterosexual couples. Between a man and a woman it is a sacrament. We don't fulfil that. To have a ceremony is a pretence. It's so sad. It's not the real thing. (John, a Church of England priest in his late 50s)

I have very clear and strong views about the differences between homosexual relationships and heterosexual relationships. I object very strongly to two people who are talking about homosexual marriage and go through marriage ceremonies. Marriage is an entirely different thing. None of that applies to homosexual relationships and therefore it's irrelevant. (Morgan, a retiree in his mid-60s)

Among respondents who are dismissive of blessing ceremonies on this ground, there is a strong negative feeling toward heterosexual marriage, which to them encompasses property and ownership, the domination and subordination model, and exclusivity.[8] Many respondents argue that instead of aping heterosexual marriage, gay couples should go beyond tradition and explore new models in the organization of their partnerships. The lack of cultural and religious guidelines in this respect affords gay couples the flexibility and freedom to explore. Ryan, an administrator in his mid-30s, represents the view of many when he argues:

It [blessing ceremony] is too heterosexual in some ways. One of the advantages of being a gay couple is that you are almost sailing in the sea of normality. Why should you take on some of the shackles of perceived normality [referring to heterosexual marriages]? It just seems a little silly to go through with it.

Related to the above point, the rejection of a blessing ceremony is also an act of defiance in the face of the absence of recognition from the Church and society at large. Unless full legal recognition follows, many believe that going through a blessing ceremony achieves nothing. There is a political dimension to this rejection of the blessing ceremony. Tom, who has been in a partnership for 16 years, argues:

No. I think it's because it [blessing ceremony] wouldn't be something that would be universally recognized. It would be a sympathetic priest who would do it, wouldn't it? And I don't want that. I mean if we were going to do anything like that, it has to be something that is formally recognized as being something that was agreed that should be done. If there was a ceremony like that in Denmark, which is a civil thing, together with the Church recognizing the validity of the relationship, I think yes I might do it. But because it doesn't, I am not interested in going through that. I think any relationship should be recognized for its worth on its own merit, and not because you sign a piece of paper. I think every marriage is a union between two people committed to each other. The priest and so on is just an outward sign.

Another primary reason for the dismissal of a blessing ceremony rests on the perceived lack of practical values. To some, a blessing ceremony does not, at this point in time, alter the legal status of the partnership. Moses, a teacher who has been in a partnership for 15 years, argues:

> I suppose if there was tax relief for [gay] married couples, we might consider it. Otherwise it fulfils no practical needs.

On the basis of the above argument, we can speculate that the number of gay couples opting for a blessing ceremony would increase if gay partnerships are religiously and legally recognized. On the other hand, some respondents argue that the duration of their partnerships is evidence of God's blessing and its commitment. A blessing ceremony is therefore not needed as further validation to their time-tested partnerships. This view is clearly expressed below:

> It [blessing ceremony] will make no difference to the relationship. Presumably, if God hasn't blessed the relationship, it wouldn't have lasted this long. (Alan, a medical professional in a 21-year-old partnership)

> I suppose a blessing ceremony is an indication about a certain degree of commitment and hope for the future. Ten years into a relationship, you should have a fair idea of the way you feel. Otherwise, you would not be together. (Nigel, a teacher in a 10-year-old partnership)

In spite of the existence of differing views between partners in a partnership in the area of blessing ceremonies, it does not prove to be a main area of contention. The couples have in general negotiated how the partnership should go in this direction. For instance, Simon and David, who have been together for 16 years, disagree on the necessity of a blessing ceremony:

> *David*: I wanted to, but he didn't want to have any sort of commitment. I wanted to do something, some sort of ceremony. But I think he was right not wanting to do that. It was just a phase really. I think it would have been silly [to have had done it]. We talked about it but nothing happened.

> *Simon*: I think we don't need a special kind of event to tie up, to mark, the relationship. It wouldn't make any difference anyway. The Church does not accept our relationship. What's the point?

David and Simon did exchange rings privately when the latter had to leave Britain for one year for work. The exchange of rings was symbolic of their commitment to each other and the partnership. On the whole, we can conclude that if gay partnerships are legally and religiously recognized, many gay couples would consider undergoing a blessing ceremony to solemnize their partnerships.

# CHAPTER 2

# Learning to Share Life Together

Falling madly in love is just a rosy start; learning to share life together is the real test. As a partnership develops, the initial limerence gradually decreases and the partners become aware of the adjustment each has to make to create impetus for the continuation of the partnership. The "honeymoon" gives way to the realization that the partnership exacts some costs as it provides awards. David McWhirter and Andrew Mattison argue that this process is typical of partnerships in the "nesting" stage, when they are between two and three years old.[1]

Learning to adjust to each other affects not only the partner's level of satisfaction, but also the stability of the partnership itself. Of course, in the case of these gay male couples, sharing life does not necessarily mean cohabitation. Forty-six of them live together, while the other 22 live apart. While some couples deliberately choose to live apart, cohabitation is not a possibility for others, owing to a myriad of factors against the arrangement. I will elaborate on this in the following section.

## LIVING ARRANGEMENTS

### Cohabiting Couples

The majority of the couples decided to live together between three months and five years after they had established their partnerships. Moving in together is not immediately possible for most primarily due to work commitments in different areas. Couples in this situation who are not too geographically distant have the tendency to see each other as frequently as possible. However, they did reach a saturation point when both felt that such an arrangement was exceedingly inconvenient and opted for cohabitation. For couples who lived far apart, strenuous effort was made to relocate one or both of their jobs in order to make cohabitation a reality.

Moses and Ron, for example, have been together for 15 years. However, cohabitation only materialized when the partnership was about 10 years old. Having begun the partnership while studying at the same university, they had to separate to teach in different places about 100 miles apart. While Moses stayed in the teaching profession, Ron left for theological training after about three years. That further separated them for another three years. Cohabitation finally became a reality when Moses relocated himself to the city where Ron worked upon completing his theological training.   Ron relates the story:

> Well, we began life together in college. At that stage, we were sort of learning the hard things as we went along. We then had to get jobs in separate places. But I mean we sort of saw each other regularly. I was teaching for three years, and then at the Bible college for three years. I mean we had very long holidays. So we were apart for a few weeks at a time. During school days we were apart, but weekends we saw each other. And then the [school] holidays, of course.

Some couples also delayed living together, although the intention was there at the initial stage of the partnerships, because of their concern about social repercussions. This is the experience of Rick and Walter, whose partnership is three years old, but they only began living together one-and-a-half years later. Rick is a priest in the Church of England. He therefore lives in the accommodation provided by the local parish church. He was concerned that Walter's moving in might raise suspicion among the parishioners about their partnership. Thus, for the first half of their partnership, they had to be content with a separate living arrangement. However this situation changed when Walter, a financial professional, had to move in later in order to take care of Rick, who had had a back operation:

> *Walter*: Really it started early last year, about a year and a half into the relationship, which is really when Rick was recovering from his back operation. I just finished a temporary assignment. So I just stayed on.

*Rick*: I needed somebody to basically do the lifting and things like that. I had back surgery and I couldn't do very much, very strenuous things. It seems sensible that he stayed here for a few weeks. He just ended up staying till now.

*Walter*: I mean we actually talked about not living together because of the flat belonging to the church and it is just around the corner. The potential difficulties with parishioners was too worrying. But at the end of the day, Rick's practical needs overrode that.

Some couples took a while before deciding to live together because of their concern about the effects of cohabitation itself. Although living separately curtails the amount of time they can spend together, the arrangement provides them with a greater degree of independence and freedom. They were concerned about losing these important elements of life. This concern for personal space is typified by Simon and John, who were together for five years before they eventually decided to cohabit:

*Simon*: When I was ready [to move in] with him, he wasn't. And then he was ready to live with me, and I wasn't. Eventually it happened that it coincided that we were both ready.

*John*: Obviously I thought I was giving up a lot of my independence by living together. Although we spent every night with each other, I still had that sense that I was as committed while I still had my own place. I could say, "Well, actually I have got someone to stay over the weekend. I'll see you on Monday." If we were living in the same house, it would be more difficult to do. Of course, subsequently we found that it isn't. It was just as easy!

### Noncohabiting Couples

Not surprisingly, most couples who do not live together actually cannot do so because of their work commitments in different parts of the country. Robert and Marcus are both Church of England priests in parishes about 100 miles apart. They have been together for almost 7 years, but only manage to meet over weekends:

*Robert*: If we want to live together, one or the other would have to change professions. That means one of us would have to give up the pastoral ministry.

*Marcus*: Well, I think in some way we are both quite keen to get out of it [the pastoral ministry] actually because of my disillusionment with the Church.

Their story highlights the difficulty of couples in which both partners are priests who have to live in accommodations provided by the parishes. Their desire to live together might never materialize as long as both remain in the pastoral ministry. Robert and Michael are also Church of England priests in different parishes about 200 miles apart. They have been together for 16 years and 6 months. They only manage to meet over weekends. They tell their story below.

*Robert*: The bottom line is, such [both of them being priests] is our lives. We have to live separately as a result. In the end it means that 16 years on we are not as far on in knowing and loving and expressing as couples who have managed to live together, because you have to learn [in a cohabiting partnership] tolerance and acceptance, and you learn to give ground. [At present] we are used to having our own space, our own ways, our own houses, and being the boss. To live together means one of us will have to give it [the pastoral ministry] up. I am not sure. That would change us and the relationship.

*Michael*: I really wish we could live together. I know that if we live together there will be a real problem because we are both used to having our own space. I expect it would take us quite some time to adjust. But I still, we both still, wish we could because we both feel instinctively that it's important to learn that. But the problem is, that means one of us will have to leave the pastoral ministry. That's the whole problem. I could think of very little opportunity in which we can be both active as priests in the same area. I don't know, but the only way that we can live together is that one of us gives up the job and takes up a secular job and lives with the other. But now it's just a dream. At the moment retirement is the only answer. But certainly we will.

Living apart is not just an option for some couples who have to keep their partnerships secret. Richard and George, whom I introduced in Chapter 1, have been together for 8 years. In their case, noncohabitation is the only viable arrangement because Richard is married and lives with his wife. George lives near Richard's home in order to facilitate their meeting on a daily basis. Inasmuch as Richard's wife also knows George and considers him a close family friend, the pressure of managing the situation is demanding to both of them, to say the least. They both think that Richard's wife does not suspect the nature of their "intimate friendship," an impression which they try very hard to manage in public.

*Richard*: My wife and I respect one another and we actually get on okay together. It might sound awful, but it's actually okay. Because I am happy now especially with my relationship with George, I can actually get on better with my wife because to be not having a relationship with George will be to deny what I am. It therefore would affect my relationship with her. [If their partnership is known], that would certainly cause me real problems because my parents wouldn't want to know me. I doubt if I would see my sons very often, and I doubt if I would see my grandson. That would just be impossible for me to cope with.

*George*: I block it out a bit. It's difficult because of being a friend to the family. That's obviously the major drawback about the whole thing. But we love each other and there is no way I want Richard's wife and the boys [Richard's children] to be hurt at all. I just couldn't handle that, and I am prepared to lie when I need to in order for our relationship to continue. I don't want him to be without the family because obviously he loves them. I couldn't handle the hurt that they would feel. So, I can live with it. You learn to live with that. I don't feel uneasy. I am not 100 percent happy about it, but I feel I can handle it and I try to be as easy as I can be. It's just a necessary evil sort of thing. But that's infinitely preferable than the hurt of the family breaking up. I don't like the lies, but I do it quite well.

Living apart is also not an option for Cliff and Michael. Although living in the same town, Cliff, a Church of England priest, and Michael, a medical professional, cannot live under the same roof. Cliff lives in church accommodation, but Michael cannot join him because they must conceal their partnership. They meet almost every day at Michael's home. They tell their story.

*Cliff*: I think the biggest problem is that I can't see myself moving in five years or so in order to do an effective job in this place. And as long as I stay in this job, it will be very difficult for us to live together.

*Michael*: I really wish that we can spend more time together. It is very difficult because as a priest he must live in the rectory. But even though I want to spend more time with him, I couldn't just rent this house out and move in with him in the rectory. It's very difficult not to have him around all the time. But there you go, we try to meet each other as much as possible.

While most couples want to live together, some deliberately choose noncohabitation. Primarily, this is to ensure that each partner has his own sufficient psychological and physical space. Warren, an editor in his mid-30s, does not want to live together with his partner despite the fact that they have been together for 13 years. He tells me:

I think I have a fear of being always absorbed into an establishment if I moved in here [his partner's house, which is larger]. You know, my flat would fit in this room or that room. So my possessions and everything would sort of vanish into the woodwork. It would be a little bit like a take-over, even though that would be entirely voluntary. And again on the pragmatic front, we have found that this [noncohabiting arrangement] works, that living apart hasn't ever really been a problem. We haven't lived in each other's pocket really since we left the university [where they met]. We have always been apart. So living apart works, particularly not to start forcing the pace.

Brian and Tony are a unique case. They are in an 8-year-old partnership. They attempted cohabitation for two years but later decided to live apart. They moved to two adjacent houses in order to be near each other and yet have their own space. I did not interview them, but both provided the following comments in the questionnaires:

At first we shared a house and then moved to adjoining terraced houses. We like to have a certain degree of independence from each other. (Brian, retiree, in his mid-60s)

I wanted my own "space" and to determine the decor and be in control of who comes to the house. I am a lover of privacy. We used to row more when we lived together. (Tony, medical professional, in his mid-40s)

The experience of Brian and Tony suggests that their decision to live separately is primarily due to their desire for more physical and psychological space, so as to reduce the potential of conflict between them. Living apart, in this case, is therefore a strategy of conflict management. Although they are an exception rather than the rule, their experience does attest to the fact that gay male partnerships have a high degree of in-built flexibility which allows the partners to modify the parameters of their partnership when the need arises in order to enhance its quality.

How often do noncohabiting partners meet? The monthly frequency of meeting varies from three days to every day. The average monthly frequency is 14 days. Obviously, the ability to meet depends on some factors that are completely beyond the couples' control, for instance, work commitments and the distance between their respective homes.

## DOMESTIC DIVISION OF LABOR

How do these couples organize the routine of domestic chores? I focus only on cohabiting couples in this case. Noncohabiting couples, due to their occasional meetings, tend not to be bogged down by the burden of household chores when they meet. Many chores such as ironing, grocery shopping, and the laundry are done independently. Of the 46 cohabiting couples, 14 of them employed domestic help. Table 1 indicates the individual respondents' views on the pattern of the division of labor.

**Table 1**
**Domestic Division of Labor with Domestic Help**

|  | Mainly done by domestic help | Mainly done by respondent | Mainly done by partner | Mainly shared equally between respondent and partner |
|---|---|---|---|---|
| Grocery shopping | 0 (0.0%) | 7 (25.0%) | 8 (28.6%) | 13 (46.4%) |
| Cleaning the house | 26 (92.8%) | 1 (3.6%) | 1 (3.6%) | 0 (0.0%) |
| Gardening * | 2 (7.7%) | 9 (34.6%) | 12 (46.2%) | 3 (11.5%) |
| Paying bills | 0 (0.0%) | 9 (32.1%) | 8 (28.6%) | 11 (39.3%) |
| Cooking | 0 (0.0%) | 8 (28.6%) | 8 (28.6%) | 12 (42.8%) |
| Washing-up | 2 (7.1%) | 6 (21.6%) | 4 (14.2%) | 16 (57.1%) |
| Laundry | 3 (10.8%) | 9 (32.1%) | 7 (25.0%) | 9 (32.1%) |
| Ironing | 5 (17.9%) | 9 (32.1%) | 9 (32.1%) | 5 (17.9%) |
| Repairs around the house | 2 (6.8%) | 6 (21.6%) | 6 (21.6%) | 14 (50.0%) |

Individual responses, N = 28
* Gardening is not applicable to one couple. The total responses is therefore 26.

Table 1 reveals that 92.8 percent of the respondents report that house cleaning is mainly done by the domestic help. All other chores, except gardening and ironing, are mainly shared equally between the partners.

As mentioned, 32 of the 46 cohabiting couples are without domestic help. Without domestic help, how do the partners themselves cope? Table 2 tells the story.

**Table 2**
**Domestic Division of Labor without Domestic Help**

|  | Mainly done by respondent | Mainly done by partner | Mainly shared equally between respondent and partner |
|---|---|---|---|
| Grocery shopping | 15 (23.4%) | 10 (15.7%) | 39 (60.9%) |
| Cleaning the house | 12 (18.8%) | 14 (21.8%) | 38 (59.4%) |
| Gardening * | 13 (30.9%) | 13 (30.9%) | 16 (38.2%) |
| Paying bills | 21  (32.8%) | 18 (28.1%) | 25 (39.1%) |
| Cooking | 20 (31.3%) | 21 (32.8%) | 23 (35.9%) |
| Washing-up | 16  (25.0%) | 10 (15.6%) | 38 (59.4%) |
| Laundry | 17 (26.6%) | 12 (18.7%) | 35 (54.7%) |
| Ironing | 19 (29.7%) | 19 (29.7%) | 26 (40.6%) |
| Repairs around the house | 21 (32.8%) | 16 (25.0%) | 27 (42.2%) |

Individual responses, N = 64
* Only applicable to 21 couples. The total responses is therefore 42.

As Table 2 indicates, the majority of respondents without domestic help report that each of the domestic chore items is shared equally between the partners. The percentage rises to as high as 60.9 percent for grocery shopping and 59.4 percent respectively for house cleaning and washing-up.

In terms of domestic division of labor, the majority of couples demonstrate either the "equality pattern" (the partners share or do the tasks together) or the "specialization pattern" (each partner specializes in different tasks).[2] While some partners are equally likely to do a specific task, some partners specialize on the basis of their personal strengths, skills, interests and work schedules. There appears to be no strict gender role specialization in this respect. Most arrive at the eventual arrangement following a trial-and-error approach, as is illustrated in the following responses:

> It [domestic division of labor arrangement] is a natural evolution. It just happened. We just assumed that it would be half and half. There is something that he is naturally more talented at. I am better at the maintenance of the house, so I will do the washing up, ironing, cleaning, and whatever. And he will tend to do major projects like decorating, although both of us will do a bit. But he will decorate in a big way and I will help. He is more a project person. It's a practical arrangement. (Alan, a priest in his early 30s)

> At the beginning, when we set up our home together, there were things that Damien [his partner] would naturally do and there would be things that I would naturally do. I suppose I was more into the housework side anyway. I would do it naturally. At that time, Damien was building up a garden. But if Damien was in the house and I was at work, he would do the things that we take for granted. If the dishes needed washing, he would just get on and do it. Basically it was just divided equally. If a job needs doing, whoever is available would do it unless it comes to more specific things like the garden, which he genuinely takes an interest in and he wants to do it himself. (Neil, a social worker in his mid-30s)

Whatever the eventual pattern, most partners go through a period of trial and error until a particular routine is established. In the process, a partner might learn new skills or unlearn previous ones to create a sense of egalitarianism.[3] Therefore, to most couples, the pattern of the domestic division of labor is not an outcome of the assumption of taken-for-granted gender roles. On the contrary, it is an outcome of a gradual development or an egalitarian decision-making.[4]

Given that both the partners are men, they do not take into the partnership taken-for-granted gender roles. Therefore, one would not feel uncomfortable about washing-up because it is perceived to be a "feminine" task, or gardening as a "masculine" task. Since both are men, they do not follow a taken-for-granted social script. What they end up doing as a routine is most likely the thing they do best, rather than what they are socialized to do.

## LEISURE ACTIVITIES

I asked each respondent to name three favorite domestic leisure activities and specify the amount of time spent on them on a weekly basis. They came up with a list of over twenty activities, with the five most popular being: (1) watching television and/or video (9.3 hours per week); (2) listening to or playing music (5.5 hours per week); (3) entertaining friends (5.8 hours per week); (4) having a conversation (11.7 hours per week); and (5) cooking and eating together (6.8 hours per week).

Four of the five most popular domestic leisure activities are pursued without the participation of a third party. This is most probably due to the lack of leisure time reported by most couples. They therefore prefer to spend the limited amount of time with each other consolidating the partnership. Entertaining friends is an important activity since gay couples can use it as a means to gain support for their partnership and to provide such support to others in the same situation. Entertaining friends at home is also a "safe" activity, compared to, for instance, participating in the gay scene, which might risk the exposure of their sexuality.

In terms of nondomestic leisure activities, the respondents identified 13 activities. The five most popular activities are: (1) going to the theater/cinema (11.8 hours per month); (2) visiting gay friends (9.9 hours per month); (3) participating in church activities (11.3 hours per month); (4) visiting heterosexual friends/ family members (11.3 hours per month); and (5) participating in the gay scene (11.2 hours per month).

## THE IMPORTANCE OF PERSONAL SPACE

The maintenance of personal space is crucial in an intimate partnership in order to avoid excessive fusion of the partners.[5] Partners maintain boundaries and regulate space within the partnership to prevent their own individuality from being subsumed into the partnership. The following response provides an accurate definition. Ryan, an administrator in his early 20s recognizes this importance despite his comparatively young partnership of one year:

You should have your own personal time, things you are able to delve into which are your time and space. So you do things that you like doing and your partner goes to do other things that he enjoys doing. And there are times you come together and share those things as well. But in order to be a complete and happy relationship, it's important that you have various interests that maybe your partner doesn't share but nevertheless respects and encourages you to do. This is not to say to have a totally private separate life, but there are other stimuli and interests in your life.

Being emotionally committed and intimate does not mean that they do not acknowledge the need to create space within the context of the partnership to which each partner can retreat. Some respondents use the development of friendships without the involvement of their partners as a means to regulate space within their partnerships. However, many couples admit that because of heavy work commitments, they prefer to spend their limited leisure time with each other.

Moses and Ron are a very busy couple. Moses is an experienced teacher with heavy responsibilities, and Ron is a Church of England priest whose pastoral profession demands a substantial amount of his time and energy. They both treasure the limited amount of free time they have together. Therefore, doing things on their own appears to be a less attractive option to them.

*Moses*: I think work is a very big part in the rest of my life. In the sense that in terms of the number of hours I work, it is quite a big part. I think for me, you know, work, my career, is the other important part of my life besides this partnership. Ron as a priest, I mean, has one day a week off. That means that our social life and time together is very much Friday evening to Saturday. Sunday isn't a day together. So therefore it does affect us.

*Ron*: I mean in the sense the only personal life that we have which is apart from each other is that which involves our work. He goes swimming on his own but that's only because I am working. I mean I don't really have much free time anyway. So I wouldn't want to spend it on my own. I think the important thing about being independent is allowing the other person to be what they are rather than actually, you know, having an independent social life. I suppose that is the case really. Saturdays is the only time we are in the house together. I mean, after an evening of fun time it's time to fall asleep, it's time to go to bed really. So we don't really have much time in a week.

The pressure of time is felt even more strongly in the case of non-cohabiting couples. The fact that they live separately gives them more time than their cohabiting counterparts to be on their own. Therefore, when there is leisure time, we can expect that they would prefer to spend all of the time with each other. For cohabiting couples, however, the need to consciously create the space is crucial, as their living arrangement allows them more time together.

Nevertheless, there are special cases. For Neil and Damien who have been together for 14 years and 3 months, they both work on shifts. This substantially curtails their time together. Therefore, when there is leisure time, they prefer to spend it together rather than apart. Neil has this to say:

> Sometimes I would like it [personal space] because I think it is an outlet. But I am not prepared to spend X amount of hours out with other people when I am not really spending enough time with Damien because of our work patterns. I think I have got personal space anyway. Because of the nature of our work and shifts, I spend a lot of time on my own and so does he. So I think compared with two people who were doing a nine-to-five job, spending time in the house every evening and every weekend I think we have got that space.

A few respondents, however, are uninterested in developing personal space. This attitude is typified by Jerry, a teacher who is in a 13-year-old partnership:

> No. I don't think I can do things on my own. I would feel churlish to do something like that. Yes, very occasionally I go to the cinema if he is working. But I feel guilty about it. Why am I at the cinema watching this film? I should be at home waiting for him to come home. It gets to me like that.

Nevertheless, most respondents told me that creating personal space is one of the most important elements to negotiate within the partnership. Why is personal space so important to them? Some say that sufficient personal space facilitates the maintenance of individuality, as argued below:

> It's a satisfactory relationship because it's a dynamic and active relationship, because it's growing, because it creates space for me to develop individually as well as with him. And I do the same for him. What is important in any relationship is to enable the other partner to have the space to grow as an individual, to empower him to do that and to create the environment for him to do that and just let them develop in terms of you. Allowing them to grow as individual people. I think that is what we have got at the moment. (James, administrator, mid-30s, 3 years and 3 months in partnership)

The above response stresses the link between individuality maintenance and relationship quality. It clearly illustrates that partners as
individuals need to draw boundaries and regulate space between
themselves. James' view is supported by the following:

> I don't cease being an individual just because I live with him.
> I mean the expression "the other half" is quite silly. We re-
> main in fact the whole. You aren't somebody's other half. The
> space that they are allowed to develop in is vital. (Simon, in a
> 14-year-old partnership)

> I believe very strongly that individuals are individuals. My
> experience is that ultimately you can't rely on somebody else
> for your own life. When you come together, I don't believe all
> of you should be subsumed in the other person. I believe
> there is a meeting of lines, but you shouldn't lose your indi-
> viduality. I think that's why the relationship can stay. I do
> some things with Francis [his partner]. But equally it is im-
> portant for me to see my friends on my own. (Jackson, in a 2-
> year-old partnership)

Many respondents claim that the lack of personal space for individuality maintenance can stultify a partnership, thus affecting its
quality adversely. James, an architect in his late 40s, has been in a
cohabiting partnership for 16 years. He asserts:

> Any couple who live with each other need the time to be by
> themselves. That's essential. So I think every partnership
> should have space like this. And I think in a partnership
> where the partners are always together, I think it is pathetic
> and dull. So I think it stimulates, I think it creates space.
> You can tell each other about what you have done and vari-
> ous interests.

Alan, a Church of England priest in his early 30s, has been with Nigel for 10 years and 2 months. He argues:

> I think I see a relationship as a secure base from which to
> develop personally. I think also, from experience, that it is
> important to have people that I can go and talk to about my
> feelings. I can talk to Nigel but there are some areas which
> are a bit difficult and threatening for him, like sexual attrac-
> tion to other people. Or just to talk about things which he is
> too closely involved to give clear help and advice. So, for in-
> stance, if he is getting angry about the way I think about the

job, it may be more sensible for me to go to people I can talk
to. They will give different sorts of angles.

Alan's argument is interesting because he does not hold the romantic
view that Nigel, as his partner, can meet all of his needs. He does not
perceive the fulfilment of his needs outside the partnership as problematic. It is also not seen as an indication of partnership decline.
This sense of pragmatism is expressed by Paul, a musician in his
late 50s, whose partnership is 16 years old.

> I think one of the most dangerous things in partnership is
> when the two people say, "Oh wow we are together!" If one of
> them dies or something, the other is totally adrift. It's awful.
> And also I think it blocks you as a person. The difference be-
> tween an immature love and a mature love is that mature
> love is two people who are both grown-ups, like two ships on
> the sea. An immature love is the one that says "I have got
> you and now all my problems are solved." That isn't true.

Alan's and Paul's views illustrate the practical expectation many
gay men bring into a partnership. This pragmatism is important for
both partners to negotiate and potentially modify the parameters of
their partnership when the needs arise. I have already demonstrated
this to a certain extent, but this theme will become more apparent as
the stories continue.

# CHAPTER 3

# War and Peace: Managing Conflict

Sharing one's life with another individual in an emotionally intimate partnership is a challenging task. The negotiation of personal space which I have addressed in the previous chapter is only one of the many issues that partners need to learn to negotiate and renegotiate. In the process of negotiation, partners experience tension or even conflict. The way in which these tensions and conflicts are handled have a significant effect on the level of satisfaction of the partnership.[1]

Interpartner conflicts and tensions are the *sine qua non* of any intimate partnership. Morgan, an experienced man in his 70s who has been in a partnership with James for 28 years, relates this point beautifully:

> I don't really think you can have two people living together in close proximity sharing the same bed and so on without any serious conflicts. It doesn't work! Two human beings who have their own lives, have their own opinions and who are reasonably intelligent and so on, there will be disagreements. You might call it "creative tension" I suppose, but I wouldn't say conflicts. We are two ordinary human beings, we are not angels. And I think we are both quite old and sensible enough to know that we shan't ever be angels and be an ideal person. We are as we are and we have to cope with it.

## SOURCES OF CONFLICT

A host of factors have the potential to generate tension and con-flict in a partnership. Some of these factors operate within the inter-nal dimension of the partnership, namely, between the partners themselves. On the other hand, factors can emerge from the external dimension when the couple relate to the outside world as individuals or a social unit.[2]

### The Internal Dimension

In the internal dimension, conflict occurs when the balancing be-tween emotional intimacy and personal autonomy is tilted off the center.[3] An individual who perceives that his partner is overde-pendent on him would consider this to be an erosion of his personal autonomy and therefore an intrusion into his personal space. Fur-ther, he also might be dissatisfied with his greater investment into the partnership in terms of time and resources. [4]

The story of Rick and Walter illustrates this point well. They have been in a cohabiting partnership for 3 years. Rick, a priest, thinks that Walter, a financial professional, is overdependent on him in the organization of their social activities. Both acknowledge that this is an unsatisfactory situation.

> *Rick*: I think I sometimes feel that I have to do a lot of the running socially. So it tends to be me that organizes the so-cial diary and me that arranges to see people. My friends tend to be his friends, but Walter doesn't have many of his own friends. So that causes a lot of tension because I feel that I am doing a lot of the work a lot of the time, which I sometimes get quite "cheesed off" about. I also feel that I'm getting resentful of all my friends being his friends. It means that if I organize anything Walter always comes too. I wouldn't mind it if Walter organized things as well that I could join in. But he doesn't. So I feel that it is a bit unbal-anced. So I want to have my own social life. I'd like to see some of my own friends on my own. Really that's it, just to have my own friends on my own.

> *Walter*: I think I don't always meet his particular needs. He spends a lot of time working on caring about other people, and consequently he needs a certain amount in return. Some-times I haven't met that in his point of view. I think that's probably the biggest source of contention. Sometimes conflicts also arise due to my tendency to neglect the outside social life

in our relationship. I do like to go out but I probably like to spend more time at home than he does. He seems to take the lead because it suits me insofar as it saves me having to make a decision. Again, one of my difficult areas is making decisions. So yes, I guess I lean on him in that respect.

Another couple experiencing the same nature of conflict is Charles and Jimmy. They have been together for one-and-a-half years, but only started cohabitation eight months before I interviewed them. They both acknowledge that they are still going through a stage of mutual adjustment.

Jimmy is a teacher. When he decided to move in with Charles, a manager, he relocated to the city where Charles has been living for a long time. He therefore has a lot to do to establish himself in the new social environment. It is exactly within this area that conflict arises for them. In Charles' view, Jimmy has not tried sufficiently hard to enlarge his own social circle, thus putting on his shoulders a heavy responsibility to manage their social diary single-handedly. This leads to the curtailment of his own social life and personal space.

Charles views Jimmy's overdependence on him as a threat to his personal autonomy. His individuality is under threat from excessive fusion. This has led him to consider the dissolution of the partnership on more than one occasion:

> I thought about it for a while because I felt he put all his problems onto me. He was relying on me all the time. He did not have any other friends whom he was relying on. He relied on me a lot. He has been in [city] for eight months and he hasn't sought to find any of his own friends at all. He hasn't gone out of the relationship to make his own friends while I came into the relationship with my own friends. So he needs to make his own friends. There is nothing wrong with that. But it really bothers me that he hasn't sought his own friends. So a lot of his social life is dependent on me. But I feel it's important in a relationship to have your own space and own friends because they can support you in times of difficulty. And that might have helped if he had his own friends to turn to. But I have a lot of friends to support me, he didn't. I was going through a lot of turmoil in my studies. He wasn't understanding how I was feeling. It went on for months and months. I just burnt out, I think. He wasn't giving me any support. He put his problem onto me. In a sense he was relying on me a lot and I couldn't give what he wanted. I just keeled over. I needed a break.

It is clear from Charles' account that Jimmy's overdependence on him has generated a substantial amount of pressure. He thinks that the responsibility has been laid unfairly on his shoulder at the expense of his own autonomy:

> It's not the ideal situation. He doesn't take the initiative on the whole. That's why I say I am more dominant in that sense. I think he likes the idea that I am being more dominant. I don't mind taking all these responsibilities. But occasionally he should take the initiative as well. So that's what annoys me sometimes.

In view of his situation, Charles expresses his sense of uncertainty for the future of the partnership:

> I think it [the survival of the partnership] depends on these elements, if there is to be any improvement. I can't go on and on, taking the initiative all the time. I think I need more space to do my own things. Like this weekend I went away to visit my mother and brother. I really enjoyed it but I can't express that to him, that I really enjoy going away. I didn't miss him as such, but I was glad to come home. I didn't really miss him when I was away. I did think a lot about him but I didn't miss him. If I have more personal space the relationship will last. The space is important because it gives the relationship the space to evaluate what's going on. I think it's important in any relationship really. You have to have your own space for your own personal development. Otherwise, what is the point of life? I think part of life is to discover yourself and to develop first of all your personhood, then secondly to develop with someone else.

Jimmy also acknowledges this conflict and the possibility of the dissolution. He knows what ought to be done. He says:

> I think that's a new area for me. But I really want to find something independent probably in the arts or maybe in the crafts side or in the computers. To give each other adequate space so that we don't stifle each other. I need to expand my social circle.

With both partners making attribution of the problem, this couple is committed to achieving a solution. They also have been to a counseling session with a gay therapist and they plan to continue with that. They also maintain that if they fail, they will still maintain their friendship after the dissolution.

The experiences of these couples testify that handling a partnership is indeed a balancing act.[5] The failure in balancing emotional intimacy and personal autonomy effectively often leads to dissatisfaction on the part of the partner who feels that his personal space has been invaded excessively.

Conflict also can take place when partners hold discrepant expectations about certain aspects of their partnership, for instance, the nature and amount of nondomestic leisure activity. Ryan and Nick who have been in partnership for one year, are learning to cope with this aspect of their partnership. Ryan, in his mid-30s, is self-employed. While he enjoys the personal autonomy and comfort of working from home, he is inclined to obscure the line between his work and his domestic life with Nick, both of which take place in the same milieu. This leads to Nick's complaint:

> Ryan works from home and he tends to work till very late at night. I really want to go out more. Sometimes I think that we are boring, and I get bored. We never really do a lot of things, you know. We tend to follow a routine. We sort of work and then on the weekends we sort of go to cinemas, you know, going out. That's about it. We just don't get out and leave [city]. Sometimes I feel choked. I need fresh air and space. I think what we need to work on is to be more spontaneous in our relationship. You know, we can just wake up and decide to go somewhere.

Conflict generated by discrepant expectations can have a serious adverse effect on a partnership. This is certainly the experience of Warren and Aaron, the editor and the priest I have already introduced. Throughout their partnership of 13 years, they have experienced two separations lasting almost two years each. The major factor that leads to the separations is the discrepancy in their mutual expectation of each other and the partnership. The situation was compounded by the fact that both of them lived in separate cities owing to their work commitments.

About six years into the partnership, Warren was convinced that Aaron did not fully meet his expectations and ideal. He found Aaron's absorption in his then first job and his low degree of self-disclosure affecting their level of intimacy adversely. His own expectations, which he now admits were unrealistic, made him feel that Aaron was not investing sufficient effort in the partnership as a result of maintaining his personal autonomy too stringently. Consequently, Warren initiated a separation.

Two years later, they met again when Aaron moved back to the same city where Warren lived. They resumed the partnership, initiated by Warren. Before long Warren again felt that the partnership

fell short of his expectations. He initiated another separation which
also lasted about two years. During that period, both had had other
relationships which failed. These failed relationships informed Warren of his unrealistic expectations of an intimate relationship. This
led to the reassessment of his relationship goals and expectations. It
was then that he reconciled with Aaron  and resumed the partnership until now. He states reflectively:

> Those failed relationships [during the separation] taught me
> quite a lot about chasing after ideals and what happens to
> ideals when they are exposed to the light of the day. When
> we met again we sort of looked at each other with new eyes,
> you know, we have both learned quite a lot. And I did change
> quite a lot. I felt that I had anyway. And still those good
> things that had always been there were sort of glimmering at
> the bottom somewhere. And it was just slowly, slowly,
> slowly, not in any terribly deliberate ways, we sort of began
> to come back together again.

These experiences have taught Warren an important lesson
about imposing his ideals on his partner and the partnership, which
resulted in the stultification of the partnership itself. He further
elaborates on the change in his perspective which is contributory to
the continuation of the partnership now:

> I think there is far more recognition of the way each of us
> works. I think in my younger years I was far more inclined to
> believe the way I thought and saw things as inevitably the
> only way to think and see things. And so I was forever want-
> ing to impose that on Aaron. Of course that was frustrating
> for me and probably confusing for him. So now we can antici-
> pate what the other one is thinking or going to say about
> something. You know, often the whole thing is dealt with by
> a glance. I think it sounds awfully dull and pragmatic, but it
> is really a matter of recognizing the qualities of, if you like,
> friendship with Aaron and partnership with him that makes
> things work. I have become less unrealistic and more prag-
> matic about the whole thing.

Aaron agrees that there has been a development of a deeper understanding between them, "I think if anything I was only being too
easy about them [relationships]. Thinking that relationships were
just something that happened. What I realize now is that it is something you have to work at. If it is worth having, it's worth working
for."

The fact that Warren and Aaron now live in the same city does facilitate their communication. However, what is more telling is the change of perspective on Warren's part especially. He, for instance, now accepts that Aaron is less expressive than he is and places greater importance on personal autonomy. He has learned to accept Aaron as a unique individual.

People grow and learn. In the process, people change. In the context of a partnership, individual changes can draw the partners closer. But they also can make them drift apart, thus generating tension that destabilizes the partnership. The story of Jackson and Francis illustrates this. Jackson, a financial professional, and Francis, a computing professional, have been together for 2 years and 3 months. They are still at the adjustment stage. Both are relatively young and at the crossroads of their careers, which pull them toward different directions. The major conflict they currently encounter is their growing incompatibility in several primary aspects of life.

There is, therefore, a need for a thorough redefinition of their relationship goals as a couple within the context of individual growth and development. Jackson needs to take examinations for career advancement which will generate great pressure on him and the partnership. Jackson relates:

> Once I get these Accounting exams out of the way, there is more there for us to hold on to. So it's worth holding on. It would be very easy for us to give up and walk away. But that doesn't solve things. So what we are trying to do at the moment is to say, "Well instead of just thinking of us as going on, what can we aim for in the short, medium and long term? Why not just accept that our relationship would change in its dynamics?" I think it's easy to think that you are living together so you are supposed to live together for five years or whatever without really thinking about it. So that's what we are trying to do at the moment. We try to understand I am doing this course. There are going to be very strong stresses at work. So our expectations of each other can be changed because in that way you are not trying to expect something that you know you can't have. It's better in my view to get that in the open.

Jackson's comment demonstrates that he adopts a rather pragmatic approach to his partnership. His pragmatism is shared by Francis:

> We were discussing where the relationship was going and what we were expecting out of it. We haven't decided to terminate it. We actually do enjoy living with each other on and off. We actually enjoy each other's company. It is not as bad

as it sounds. I think we have reached a kind of stalemate and ask, "Where do we go from here?" Our relationship is definitely going through a transition right now. Partly we are growing in different directions, we are both changing at the same time but we are not sure which way we are going.

Both Jackson and Francis expressed their uncertainty in the interview about the survival of the partnership. However, they are committed to achieving a solution, even if it changes the dynamics of their partnership. The nature of the partnership will change with the redefined boundary, as Jackson relates:

I am expecting Accountancy exams in two weeks' time and I have already applied for a job. If I pass the exams, then I will study for the finals. That will mean the stresses that were present before will come back. But we have discussed the fact that we ultimately want the relationship to succeed, but it will be on a different plane with different terms. I don't know if it will actually be different but it is just that we acknowledge that there will be stress and therefore expectations have to be changed. We have also said that the basis for all this is trust and honesty. You have to be truthful about what you do because if you are not there is no point. I think it is essential to all relationships. They all have difficult times.

The prospect of the dissolution of their partnership does not deny them the hope that they can still remain friends even if the partnership fails to continue. Both are hopeful about the maintenance of their friendship:

*Jackson*: There is no animosity, which I am very grateful for. I think it says a lot about us as a couple as well, that we don't have rows. We might have disagreements though.

*Francis*: I think the thing is unless we estrange, even if we split up, I don't think it would be a real split. I think we will still remain friends. I don't think we will end up being enemies.

Their pragmatism reflects their positive attitude. The possible dissolution of the partnership might generate disappointment, but it might also lead to the enhancement of their personal identities as individuals, which, at this juncture of their lives, seems to be more integral to them than their social identity as a couple.

## The External Dimension

A partnership involves not just the individuals, but also the social world outside the partnership. A couple is not separated from the
wider social network since their existence as a social unit is located
within it. In this connection, one of the major issues the couple need
to negotiate is the extent to which others are included or excluded in
their partnership. Achieving the right balance between the extent of
inclusion and exclusion ensures the couple the availability of support
and the minimization of intrusion.

This is especially true for the sexual dimension of a partnership.
Major conflicts can threaten the stability of the partnership when
partners hold different expectations in the area of sexual exclusivity.
I will discuss this issue more extensively in Chapter 5. At this point,
I will use the story of Richard and George to illustrate the conflict
that can exist in this sensitive area.

Richard is a civil servant in his late 40s. George, also a civil servant, is in his late 30s. They have been together for 8 years. Richard
is a dominant person and George is inclined to pander to his demands. Having had a short period of exclusive partnership, Richard
urged George to participate in sexual experimentation with others.
George complied. They soon were involved in a lifestyle of frequent
casual sexual contacts. Their ground rule for sexual experimentation
was that they could not bring any casual sexual partners home in
each other's absence.

George, however, soon lost his interest in this lifestyle. Nevertheless, this lifestyle persisted owing to Richard's insistence and
George's inability to articulate his views and desire to please.
George's continued silence encouraged Richard's overdominance. The
consequence was disastrous, as Richard relates:

> I think the way was that, I just told him what I wanted and
> I didn't listen to what he wanted. And because he knew I
> wasn't going to listen he wouldn't tell me. So therefore if I
> wanted to go somewhere I just said, "I want to go there." And
> he wouldn't argue because he would just accept that it was
> what I wanted to do and I was not prepared to negotiate,
> and I wouldn't ask him what he thought because I didn't
> really value what he thought. So I would just do whatever I
> wanted, and he tagged along. He was just like a sheep really.
> I just wasn't that interested in him and he thought that I
> wasn't treating him with respect and love. He said he needed
> to be held and comforted and be close to someone, and I
> wasn't really that close to him. We had sex fairly often, we
> had sex with other people, but it wasn't working I think, to

the extent that it was really building on a false premise to start with.

George agrees, also acknowledging his own presumptuousness as partially responsible for the decline and breakdown of their partnership:

> Basically it got to the stage where I, for a while, hadn't actually been saying how I felt about things because of the situation we got into where I had been telling white lies about specific things that I didn't really like: sexual ventures with other people and things like that. I knew that he liked that and I liked it initially but I did go off it. But I didn't have the courage to tell him. So the lie perpetuated itself. So it just carried on and I just carried on telling white lies and suffering inside. I just couldn't cope. I just didn't feel particularly loved I suppose. You just get to the stage where I suppose you are sort of in a rut. You do things initially because they were sort of exciting but then I don't really have the courage to say I don't want this anymore. Perhaps that was due to the fear of losing him, because if he wanted it so much, then he might not want me anymore because I was not prepared to have threesomes or something. So I carried on doing it. But you just suddenly find yourself in situations where you are doing things that you don't really want to do but you don't have the courage to say it. It's a very sad state to be in.

It is clear that George's silence encouraged Richard to disregard his feelings. This resulted in relationship decline and George's search for love and comfort outside the partnership. This development is acknowledged by both of them:

> *George*: So I met someone. I just happened to meet someone for sex, but it developed a bit further than that because the person was giving me what I felt I wasn't getting from Richard, which is the care and attention. A bit of caring basically, a bit of what I thought might be love, but it wasn't. I think it's the fact that someone would listen to me talking and I could be honest from the beginning without having to cover myself with silly lies or whatever.

> *Richard*: It became apparent that in fact George was just looking for someone who cared for him. I obviously wasn't caring for him and therefore when this person came on the scene and was obviously prepared to care for him, he went with him, although he picked him up just for sex initially. When

the person showed him an interest, George obviously became interested because someone was talking to him in the way that I didn't talk to him.

George's search for love led him to taking the man concerned home, thus breaking the ground rule of the couple's arrangement. When Richard learned about this, the stability of the partnership was threatened. Richard viewed the incident as a betrayal of trust. It effected a thorough reassessment of their partnership. This led George to consider the importance of articulateness on his part to improve mutual communication:

> I mean to actually open my mouth and say what is going through my mind. A number of times I sat there as I was driving along thinking things, but not saying them for whatever reasons. I really need to actually say what is going on in my mind, and give Richard the opportunity to answer the questions in my mind. Everyone keeps talking about communicating, it's bloody important, it really is. If you communicate with your partner, then you can come to an understanding about things. Basically what I have learned is that you can't just get complacent in relationships. You have to carry on and both work at it, even after eight years of doing silly things.

The story of Richard and George illustrates the adverse effect on the partnership when both partners have discrepant expectations about the manner in which they, as a couple, ought to relate to the outside social world. Sexual exclusivity is only one of the many issues that a couple have to address. Of course, in their case, their lack of effective communication was also a contributory factor to the difficulty they encountered. They, as I will discuss in Chapter 5, have now reverted to an exclusive arrangement.

## Some Observations

In the main, there seems to exist no role conflict in the couples I interviewed. I would argue that since there are no fixed role orientations in a gay male partnership, the possibility of departure from conventional role expectations that would generate conflict is nonexistent. Not having a social script, a couple needs to negotiate and renegotiate their roles in the partnership.

Couples facing conflicts that threaten the stability of the partnerships are generally young. I speculate that they, having time on their side, are less inclined to "settle down" unless they are highly satisfied with the current partnership. Their partnerships are also comparatively young, ranging from one-and-a-half to two-and-a-quarter years. These couples are undergoing a period of transition which requires them to redefine and reassess both their individual and their partnership goals.

Contrary to what some researchers comment,[6] these couples are not in the typical "honeymoon" stage despite their young partnerships. Their partnerships are not characterized by a high degree of limerence, or being in love to the extent of being insensitive to each other's weaknesses. I would argue that this is due to their commitment to the partnership and their desire to lay a solid foundation for its further development. By the same token, it can be argued that the beginning of the partnership can be a difficult time as both partners are committed to adjusting to each other and relating to the wider social network as a social unit.

Far from being a honeymoon year, the first year can be a difficult period of adjustment when both partners are committed to working at the partnership instead of adopting a wait-and-see attitude. This can lead to conflict and even the thought of dissolution of the partnership when it is not going according to one's expectation. This is the experience of many couples, as is succinctly expressed below:

> I don't think about it [the dissolution of partnership] very often now at all. But in the early days I certainly did. I mean in the first year I was thinking about it every week. I think we were committed to the relationship. I think we both recognized that we need a relationship and both of us have spent a long time on our own which neither of us particularly likes. So the relationship became something to really work at and preserve. [Relationships] can be difficult. You have to work at them in order to make them succeed. (Rick, in a 3-year-old partnership)

Another observation is the existence of a large amount of room for reassessment and negotiation within these partnerships. Many respondents view their partnerships as a dynamic interactional process. A partnership is alive and dynamic. Both partners need to recognize that and develop as individuals within the partnership:

> I think we both see the relationship as a continuing, a very dynamic thing. And so far in the years we have known each other, that has certainly been the case. Things change, our thoughts change, our ways of dealing with things and each other change. Our priorities, our ideals, plans are just continuously changing. So we are continually developing person-

ally and together; and enabling and empowering each other to develop. (James, in a 3-year-old partnership)

The comment above attests to what I have already argued, that the flip side of the lack of institutional support and affirmation for gay partnerships is the abundance of freedom and flexibility in boundary negotiations. Partners can constantly negotiate the partnership's constitutional arrangement and redefine the boundaries within which the partnership operates to the satisfaction of both partners. Jackson and Francis are an example *par excellence*.

## CONFLICT MANAGEMENT

Different individuals respond to a conflictful situation in a myriad of ways. Their responses, however, have significant effects on the partnership. Some individuals actively discuss the situation, which leads to a constructive solution that strengthens the partnership. Some, having discussed the situation, decide to dissolve the partnership. On the other hand, some respond with inaction, which leads to passive acceptance of the status quo. Inaction may also lead to relationship breakdown. Caryl Rusbult calls these responses "Voice," "Exit," "Loyalty," and "Neglect" respectively.[7]

These partnerships have survived despite the existence of conflict. What are some of the primary means these couples use to manage the tension and conflict that emerge in their partnerships? Most couples consider effective communication the most important conflict management strategy. While it does not eliminate the emergence of conflicts altogether, effective communication ensures that the partners tackle the conflict and identify a solution concertedly.

Communication between partners is of paramount importance to the survival of partnerships. Lawrence Kurdek reports that nonresponsiveness (no communication and support between partners) is the main reason for the dissolution of gay couples.[8] On the other hand, Matthew Modrcin's and Norman Wyers' study of gay couples also reveals that the improvement of communicative skills constitutes the major type of professional help that they seek.[9] In the same vein, other researchers stress the importance of "real talk" between partners, which facilitates a process of effective negotiation for the constitutional arrangement of the partnership.[10] Indeed, the importance of effective communication cannot be over-emphasized.

James and Nigel have been together for 3 years and 3 months. Their commitment to effective communication has helped enhance their partnership:

*James*: There aren't any major conflicts. The potential for major conflict is there definitely, as in any relationship. It has got to be. But it is because we respect each other. We don't make major decisions without consulting with each other. I don't think we disrespect each other enough not to involve each other in the decision-making. We always communicate. And if we don't, it becomes so obvious that we haven't. And that will bring us to a point where we do, because we are so aware that that's what's going on. So that enables us to live much closer to the borders, or the frontiers of what a relationship means and what spirituality means. Because we are able to communicate, therefore we have got security with each other, rather than keeping the "security" of either possessing each other or controlling each other which gives you a very false sense of security and control.

*Nigel*: No [there are no major conflicts], because we communicate. It's not in the nature of our relationship to have major tensions because very early on if there is a single doubt or discontent, then we talk about it. No, I don't think we have any major conflicts. We never get to the stage of disagreement because we communicate about our desires before we decide on anything. We never get that far down in the decision-making process when we have diametrically opposed views because we deal with it as we start to diverge. I would say effective communication is the key to why we have our relationship in the first place. It's that deep deep communication that drew us together in the first place and it established the things we have. We have a deep need to communicate, to understand, to be understood. So that's where we get our energy from.

Effective communication is indisputably important in providing the opportunity for the partners to analyze and attempt to resolve a conflict.[11] It also helps the partners to make attribution individually and collectively in order to give causal explanations to a conflictful event. Making attribution identifies the fundamental cause of a conflict and facilitates the construction of an effective solution. Conversely, the lack of communication might lead to "attributional ambiguity and avoidance," which can lead to relationship breakdown.[12]

Of course, the effectiveness of communication should improve as the partnership develops. The growing familiarity between partners helps diffuse the potential of conflict.[13] Michael, a priest who has been in a partnership for 16 years and 6 months, has this to say:

I think we argue less now than we used to, quite simply because there is more confidence there, having survived for so many years. Robert [his partner] doesn't see everything that I say as an attack. So I think it causes less and less friction. This is not because we have grown apart, but because I think the foundation of love and affection grows stronger and awareness of what each of us contributes to the relationship grows.

Morgan and James, on the other hand, have been together for 28 years. They have learned to communicate effectively and hold realistic expectations of each other:

*Morgan*: Well I think we communicate really well. Sometimes like all sensible people one can get into an argument ... Oh well, I would like him to be tidier, I would like him to agree with me on a lot more points, get him to think. We argue about the Presbyterian Church and the Anglican Church. We have disagreements about opera. I love the operas of Wagner for example and he doesn't like that and is against that kind of thing. Nothing I would call conflicts exactly. I think if we had conflicts then we wouldn't be together.

*James*: Well I am sure he has gone on about my drinking so I shall go on about his smoking. We are both slightly addicted to things, I mean habits, and I think we both hate being reminded of them. I have always felt that one of my major failures with him was to stop him from biting his nails. I don't think there is anything I dislike about him apart from his obsessive tidiness, which is a thing that I object to and he has undoubtedly said about my untidiness. He's also a very bad passenger, and he shouts about my driving and how I miss traffic lights and how I'm not getting on fast enough and all the rest of it. I am so used to it I don't take the slightest notice. If there were one small thing that I would like to improve in this relationship that would be that he behaves himself in the car! But because we have been in this relationship for so long now, the things that are annoying are no more than little annoyances like midges or that sort of thing that gets in the way of perfection.

Another way to prevent and manage conflict is to maximize the opportunity of joint decision. This is closely related to effective communication. Effective communication does facilitate a joint decision-making process. Moses and Ron, who have been together for 15 years, consider this an important ingredient for a successful partnership.

> *Moses*: Yes, I won't do anything if I feel it is going to cause a problem. Like going on holiday, we would decide together. I mean, it took several months of just talking about where we are going to go on holiday this year. In the end we came up with something which we both agreed with. I guess what you probably do in fact is that you might fly an idea casually and see how it goes back. Then perhaps raise it again at another good time and see what the response is. Then perhaps on the third time you should get quite serious about this and then, you know, things then begin to happen. I mean if Ron suggests something which sounds like a good idea, then I'll probably say yes.

> *Ron*: I should say that we don't really make big decisions alone. I mean, inasmuch as these things count, I don't think there are particularly clear roles. I think some people would try the female roles and the male roles within relationships. I don't think we are in that case you see. But then again, after such a long time of being together, there isn't much talking to do because there will be no point for me to suggest something which I knew wouldn't be acceptable. I know what is what and what isn't, and so there would be no point in making suggestions to him which I knew he wouldn't accept. I think to an outsider it would possibly look as if, because I am slightly more vocal or forceful, it might be me who makes decisions. But at the end of the day it actually isn't because I know exactly where the boundary is and so you get that sort of silence which you don't cross over. You actually just want to carry on with the relationship. I mean there is no point in suggesting something which I know won't be acceptable.

The commitment to equality, manifested in joint decision-making, is prevalent among these couples.[14] James and Nigel, who place great emphasis on effective communication as I have mentioned, illustrate this commitment.

> *James*: I think one of the major strengths of our partnership is that we make decisions together and if either of us ever feels that one or the other has made a decision which hasn't been an equal decision, then we will say so. [With reference to his 13-year seniority] Well I guess it could give me an advantage in decision-making because of my years of experience or whatever. So there are some decisions which that experi-

ence is appropriate, then it may give me the edge. It may give me more information but I don't think Nigel would accept that. There are other decisions, anything to do with figures, for example, then he is streets ahead of me. So he brings his experience of knowledge to bear in that. So I suppose we try to allow each other space. I think both of us have different strengths, but most decisions are actually very consensual and it doesn't feel to me like, even with my extra years of experience, I have the edge, because I think I would be very sensitive to that ... I don't feel that that's a feature of our relationship at this stage.

*Nigel*: Well, we bring different things to the partnership because we have had different experiences and because we are different. But we still make decisions together. One of the dynamics of our relationship is that because of my youth I bring different angles to things than he does. So his age does not give him the advantage. We bring different things and we make our decisions based on them.

The stories of the couples I have presented thus far prove that the existence of potential and actual conflict is inevitable in a partnership. However, it is not the existence of the conflict, but the way it is managed that determines its impact on the partnership. The commitment to and practice of effective communication and egalitarian decision-making appear to be the key means of achieving positive results.

## PARTNERSHIP SATISFACTION AND EXPECTATION

In the interviews, I asked each respondent to rate, on the scale of 1 to 10, his level of satisfaction with his partnership. The higher the rating, the greater the satisfaction. On the whole, 93.2 percent of the respondents give a rating of 8 or higher in this connection. With a mean rating of 8.8, this indicates in general that there is a high level of satisfaction among the respondents, despite the presence of conflicts in their partnerships. There are several reasons for this high level of satisfaction. The primary reason is the rewards of being in a partnership:

I think this relationship has sort of made me confront those areas of my personality that weren't functioning very well. You know, the relationship and the things that have come out of the relationship have been a source of strength to me. I mean this is certainly one of the things that I value very much about the relationship. It has done that for me. (Walter, a financial professional in a 3-year-old partnership)

I mean I feel really quite happy. I think it [the partnership] is probably the biggest achievement in my life. I mean what I've achieved in terms of exams or career, I don't think they match up. I think I am extremely lucky. I doubt that there is anybody who is really happier in a relationship. What I have got now, what I've achieved now, I value it. I don't particularly want to lose it. (Moses, a teacher in a 15-year-old partnership)

Except young couples such as Charles and Jimmy, and Jackson and Francis, whom I have already discussed, the majority expect their partnerships to last until one of the partners passes away. Some respondents are very confident about the longevity of their partnerships, as expressed below:

I mean if he came tomorrow and said that he was going to leave me, I mean I would be just so astounded. I don't know what I would do. I just can't believe it could ever happen. I am so confident. I have total confidence in him in terms of two in one flesh, as Christians say. I really have that confidence. (Samuel, in a 27-year-old partnership)

This confidence emanates from a great sense of certainty about their mutual commitment. Entering into a partnership and developing it with mutual understanding and common goals appears to be the basis of this confidence:

Yes, that [to be together until death] is the intention and we have made wills with that intention. We have talked about the fact that we are totally committed to each other for the length of our shared life. That's our intention. We never want to go through the pain of splitting up. So we will work to stay together. And that is in the sense a duty on each other because it is a costly thing to promise to your partner that you will be faithful with the understanding that the other is doing the same thing. But we said that should anything happen to either of us and the other be left widowed, then the other would be free to start living again with a new partner or whatever. So it is till death do us part. That is definitely our commitment. I mean we have formalized that in a ceremony. (Calvin, in a 5-year-old partnership)

This issue of the longevity of the partnership brings about the issue of death. This proves to be a matter of concern for certain couples with  a vast age difference. For Ricky, who has been in a partnership for 27 years with Samuel, who is 23 years his senior, the presumed earlier death of Samuel is a matter of concern:

The thing that worries me is death and the fact that perhaps he may die before me. It does concern me a bit. It is there at the back of my mind. But obviously I don't dwell on it every day, but it is a factor. I realize that I have to come to terms with it and be prepared for it.

In spite of the presence of conflicts, these couples demonstrate a high level of satisfaction with their partnership. The majority also expect their partnerships to last until death. Eighty-nine of the 136 respondents who participated in my study have drawn up wills, and 84 of them named their partners as the sole or primary beneficiaries. Many of them also have other financial arrangements for each other in the event of death. This outlines their satisfaction with and commitment to life-long partnerships. It also repudiates the stereotype that gay men are incapable of and uninterested in establishing long-term partnerships.

## FORMULA OF SUCCESS

I have clearly demonstrated by now that these couples are highly satisfied with and committed to their partnerships in spite of the tensions and conflicts they experience, as any couple would when two individuals relate to each other intimately. The durations of these partnerships  range from 1 to 33 years, with an average of 9 years and 5 months. This is undoubtedly a very impressive feat, in view of the lack of social support and religious affirmation.

What contributes to the success of these partnerships? This question has been indirectly answered when I discussed how these couples minimize and manage the tension and conflict in the partnerships. Here, I will elaborate further on some of the "recipes" the couples I interviewed shared with me.

A coupled relationship, like any other intimate relationship, is not a static entity. Rather, it is an ongoing process in which the partners must continuously learn to manage and develop. Complacency destroys many intimate relationships; hard work keeps them alive and lets them flourish. The recognition and willingness to embrace change in the partnership is therefore an important task that the partners need to master. Change need not be a threat, although by its nature it might have some destabilizing effect on the partnership initially. But with the partners' commitment, this change will only serve to further strengthen the partnership as it adapts and evolves.

Change is a healthy development within a partnership to ensure that it is not stultified by the routine of everyday life. It is therefore important for partners to treat their partnerships as a dynamic process and keep working at it. Complacency is what the partners must fight hard to keep at bay. Rick, the priest, and Walter, the financial professional, have been learning to effect some positive changes in their partnership. I have already mentioned that Rick feels that he is quite tired of the role of the "leader" or "organizer" in their social life. Walter, on the other hand, acknowledges that he must learn to make more decisions and be more expressive. In fact, he started seeking professional counseling for a couple of years before I interviewed him. Both of them have also planned to seek couple counseling to enhance their partnership. They tell me their story below:

> *Rick*: I think the fact that the relationship has survived [despite the difficulty] probably says something about the quality of it, although we don't feel we are in seventh heaven. But I think we both probably feel we can support each other because life has been pretty tough for us in the last few years. We hope it will get easier in the future.

> *Walter*: [In terms of improvement] I think my ability to perhaps contribute more to the social side of the partnership. Probably our sex life could also be improved. A lot of it is bound up in me feeling sort of more confident and happy with myself as a person. I probably need first to actually bring that improvement to the relationship.

Of course, not all changes are welcomed by both partners. Partners might even disagree about the kinds of changes they wish to see in the partnership. Compromise, then, becomes an important feature. Nobody in a relationship can have his needs and expectations fulfilled completely. It is therefore important to have realistic expectations and learn to compromise. Warren, the editor, and Aaron, the priest, are a good example. I have told their story at length earlier in this chapter. Having experienced two separations, they both have learned to compromise. Similarly, Alan and Jon, who have been together for 21 years, seem to have learned this lesson well.

> *Alan*: We could do with being a little more open in discussing things. But I hate discussing things, personal things. So we don't. But it would be a very good idea I suspect if I didn't hate it so much and we were a bit more open. But I have a strong aversion to deep personal discussions of my own feel-

ings. I would find it extremely difficult to go to a psychotherapist or counselor. Very difficult, I don't like it at all. We do
discuss things, but only in passing.

*Jon*: I think it has always been like that; I think it would
probably survive whichever. I think perhaps we could avoid
some pain on both sides maybe if we discussed a bit more.
But I think you always have to work on the verges of compromise. Yes, compromise is definitely a key word. On the
whole, we don't discuss very much, we just sort of vaguely
know what will work and what won't.

In the area of self-disclosure, Jon has to compromise with Alan's
lack of expressiveness. However, in the area of sex, it is Alan's turn to
compromise. They do not make love together anymore. Alan knows
fully well that Jon has casual sexual encounters outside the partnership. He accepts that with a strict ground rule that Jon must follow:
such encounters must not take place at home in his presence. This
will be elaborated on further in Chapter 5. Suffice it to say at this
point that each partner has to learn to give and take in order to balance the costs and rewards of being in a partnership.

One of the positive things about the duration of a satisfying
partnership is that the partners mutually build a common relationship history which becomes a significant part of their personal social
biographies. This common history serves as a bond that cements the
partnership. Damien and Neil, who were in the fifteenth year of their
partnership when I interviewed them, have this to say:

*Damien*: Now one of the things that I suppose keeps you together is that you think, well we've been together for such a
long time. We've shared so many things. We've been through
so many things. We have helped each other. There have been
times when Neil has been unemployed and I've been ill, and
he has been ill and I've been unemployed. We've always
shared everything right down the middle. I've never kept a
secret penny for myself, and Neil has never done that. All
that effort you put into it, you've got to consider that. It's got
to have some meaning, you just don't throw the whole lot
overboard. Maybe in a way the longer you are together the
more difficult it becomes to separate. Of course, you grow into
each other. We know each others' faults and failings and so,
you know, you are always learning something new anyway.

*Neil*: Yes, you do grow into each other. You do realize some-
how that you grow closer, you grow more like somebody. You
tend to take on somebody's good characteristics. I feel I've

got, I couldn't tell you what, but I've got bits of him. I could tell you, "Yes, he has got this and that quality that I've taken because I liked it." I think I could get more from him because he's older and he has had more experience.

"Growing into each other" is a beautiful phrase. It denotes that the partners' shared experiences in the partnership serve as a common bond. However, in order to prevent stultification of the partnership, the partners also need to be wary of not growing too much into each other. This is where personal space comes into the picture. I have already discussed in Chapter 2 the importance of maintaining personal space for most couples.

Maintaining and managing tension and conflict in an intimate relationship is never easy, given that individuals entering into such relationships increasingly place emphasis on personal satisfaction and fulfilment.[15] However, in the words of Aaron, the priest, "If it's worth having, it's worth working for!"

# CHAPTER 4

# What Is Yours Is Mine, What Is Mine Is Ours?: Financial Arrangements

Work and money are essential aspects of a man's identity. Having a career and financial independence are crucial to a man's masculinity. This is a result of socialization that affects the majority of men, heterosexual and gay alike. Therefore, most gay men are not happy being homemakers, or being dependent on their partners. Philip Blumstein and Pepper Schwartz, for instance, report that most gay couples believe that both partners should work. Hence, it can be expected that, under normal circumstances, virtually all gay couples are dual-career.[1] Interpartner economic parity is also a prominent issue for gay male couples.[2] In this chapter, I will discuss how these couples organize their finances and manage this sensitive dimension of their partnership.

## FINANCIAL MANAGEMENT

The majority of the couples, particularly the noncohabiting ones, adopt the "separate management style," in which both partners keep their finances completely separate from each other. A minority of couples opt for the "partially separate management style," in which the couples maintain financial independence but keep a joint account for various purposes, mainly to cover common expenditures. An even smaller minority manage their finances with "complete pooling," in which both partners completely combine their financial resources.[3]

### Separate Management Style

Why manage their finances separately? Most couples say that this management style is precipitated by the desire to maintain financial independence. A good example in this case is Ricky and Samuel. Both retired, Ricky has an annual pension of between £5000 and £8999, and Samuel between £21000 and £24999. They bought a car together, although it is registered in Ricky's name. They also name each other as the primary beneficiaries in their life insurance policies and wills. Nevertheless, this cohabiting couple of 27 years have always maintained separate individual accounts. They tell their main reason for this arrangement in the questionnaires.

*Ricky*: We both have different sources of income. I prefer to have some financial independence.

*Samuel*: We prefer the independence of separate accounts.

More than two-thirds of the noncohabiting couples manage their finances separately, citing their living arrangement as the primary reason for this scenario. Warren and Aaron typify this situation. They have been together for 13 years but live separately, because they want to maintain some personal space. Warren, an editor in his mid-30s, has a gross annual income of between £170000 and £20999. On the other hand, Aaron, a priest in his mid-30s, earns between £9000 and £12999 annually. They do not jointly own any properties. Unlike Warren, Aaron has drawn up a will and a life insurance policy. However, Warren has not been named as a beneficiary.

Under normal circumstances, they would meet over the weekend, mainly at Aaron's home. They both consider that their living arrangement warrants the separate management of their finances:

*Warren*: Since we do not, as a rule, live together, a joint account [to manage finances jointly] would be unhelpful to say the least.

*Aaron*: As we don't live together, we have separate outgoings to settle.

How, then, do these couples settle joint expenditures, such as domestic bills and food, particularly in the case of cohabiting couples? Most of them tend to settle common expenditures by each partner making an equal contribution. By splitting the expenditure down the middle, a sense of balance and equality is achieved. Neither feels that he is dependent on his partner or being dependent upon. Rick is a Church of England priest, with an annual income of between £13000 and £16999. His partner, Walter, a temporary financial professional, has an annual income in the £5000-£8999 bracket. Although they have been together for three years, they have always maintained financial independence. Rick explains how the system works for them:

> We have never felt the need [to pool their finances]. I pay all the bills from my own account and my partner simply gives me a cheque for 50 percent.

Similarly, Sam and David, a cohabiting couple who have been together for 7 years, also manage common expenditures in this way. Both Sam, a social worker, and David, a manager, earn between £13000 and £16999 annually. They jointly own a house, and have drawn up wills in which they name each other as the main beneficiaries. However, they manage their incomes separately. They also rule out the need of a joint account to pool their financial resources:

> *Sam*: We pay bills through our own accounts and ensure that it balances at the end of each month. So, it works out 50-50.

> *David*: Where bills and expenses are recorded and settled monthly, a joint bank account is a totally unnecessary complication.

Nevertheless, some couples do not follow a rigid 50-50 guideline in covering their joint expenditures. The partners tend to cover different expenses at different times at random. However, they ensure that a sense of equality is maintained in order that neither feels overburdened. Morgan and James are in this situation. Both retired, Morgan has a gross annual income of between £25000 and £28999, while James is in the £17000-£20999 bracket. They maintain financial independence from each other, and thus see no need for a joint account. They do not operate a strict system. They pay for expenditures on a random basis but are mindful of the importance of equality.

This couple have been together for 28 years. They jointly own a house and a piece of land. They have also drawn up wills with each other as the main beneficiaries. They explain how their system works:

> *Morgan*: The system just evolved, you see. James was in this house about a year before I joined him. So he sort of got into the habit of paying the bills for the electricity and so on. And then we did various things and he goes on doing that because

it's all in his name and so on. And every so often he says he is short of money and I give him £1000 or something. On the other hand, I generally pay for the holidays. I pay for the cleaning lady. So it works out roughly fifty-fifty. I couldn't give you a balance sheet because we don't do anything like that, but it's roughly fifty-fifty. You see, we have all got our own interests. For example, there are a whole range of charities that James supports and a quite different range that I support. He buys various things and I buy various other things. I mean I like books and so on. So no, we have never seen any point in a joint account at all.

*James*: We both know that his income is bigger than mine now and that he tends to pay for certain things and I tend to pay for other things. I normally pay certain elements of the Barclay Card bill, like petrol and drinks. But if I am having a bad month, well then he just pays that bill. He tends to pay for holidays and I pay for the car, and I pay for drinks and food. But on balance I think we have both recognized that if I'm feeling broke then I just say, "Pay this one," and he will. So yes, I think we do accept that fifty-fifty is what we want it to be but very rarely do I ever try and work the expenses out.

There are, however, couples who do not share common expenditures on a 50-50 basis. This is usually due to the vast difference in the partners' earnings. The partner who earns substantially more tends to make a larger contribution to settling common expenditures. Simon and John typify this situation. They are in a 14-year-old partnership and they have been cohabiting for 9 years. John's annual income as an administrator is in the region of £5000 to £8999. Simon, on the other hand, earns between £25000 and £28999 per annum as a musician. Although they initially attempted to share common expenditures on an equal basis, it did not take too long before both of them realized that it was not a plausible arrangement.

Hence, they developed a "proportional contribution" system. Since Simon earns about one-quarter of John's salary, he makes a 25-percent contribution to cover the common expenditures. They explain this development, which initially had its own difficulty.

*Simon*: Well he earns about four times as much as I do. So we pay the same percentage of what we earn. That was something we worked out because initially that was a difficult area. It has something to do with my pride, I think. I mean it would have been very nice to have gone in equally on that, but that isn't possible without a big change in the way we live. [Now] it seems to work very well. I mean I don't mind anymore. I've got to the stage where it's hardly thought about.

*John*: Yes, money caused trouble to us initially. I had this job at [place] when I was still very young and it had a very good salary straight away. So straight away I found myself able to afford all sorts of things that I had never imagined that I was able to afford. When I met Simon he was still hanging on to his studentship. And he finds it difficult to stop being a student. I also think he saw me as rather middle class. But we managed to sort the money thing out by making it proportional, so that if a third of my income went on paying for things, a third of his should too. He wasn't very happy about it to start with because he wanted to match it pound for pound, which was of course nonsense. But I thought that it's the same hardship to him as it is to me, in proportion to what we are earning. Then he sort of went along with that. For me the most valuable thing is that we live together. It'd be silly to fall out over money.

Paul and John are in the same situation. They do not live together, although they meet almost every day. Paul earns between £13000 and £16999 per year as a priest. John is also a priest, but he has a private income which increases his total annual income to more than £32000. Given the vast difference in their incomes, John agrees to cover 75 percent of the expenditures incurred when they are together. He says:

I am the one with money. But it never interferes with our relationship because we don't allow it to interfere. He accepts the arrangement and he doesn't feel belittled or anything. It's a case of giving and taking. You have got to learn to give. I give more because I have more. That's all.

Whether equal or unequal contributions are made by both partners to settle common expenditures, it is clear that these couples prefer to manage their finances separately in order to maintain individual financial independence. Pooling financial resources together does not appeal to them. They also do not see the need to have a joint account in which money for settling common expenditures can be deposited. This seems to be particularly true for noncohabiting couples.

## Partially Separate Management Style

Couples in this case maintain partial financial independence by opening a joint bank or building society account. Each partner makes a contribution to the joint account, through which common expenditures such as domestic bills are settled. Some, however, save money in the joint account specifically to finance their annual vacation. Most of these joint accounts were opened within three years after the partnerships had been established.

Why do they want a joint account and yet maintain a certain degree of financial independence? Convenience seems to be the main motivating factor for this scenario. Alan and Jon, a cohabiting couple who have been together for 21 years, are a good example. Alan, a medical professional, earns an annual income of between £13000 and £16999. On the other hand, Jon's annual income as a manager is more than £32000. They jointly own a house and some shares in a business. They have also drawn up wills and life insurance policies that name each other as the main beneficiaries. Asked why they hold a joint account to manage common expenditures, Alan answers:

> It's convenient. It saves constant accounts and repaying each other small sums. If either of us goes shopping, we take the joint bank account cheque book with us to pay for the shopping. We each put equal amounts into the account and have our own private accounts as well. So if there is a gas bill or an electricity bill to be paid, we use the money from the joint account.

In addition to convenience, a joint account also is viewed as a symbol of commitment to some couples. The questionnaire data below illustrate this point:

> A joint account underlines the sense of partnership. (Kieran, a manager, in partnership for 18 years)

> Convenience and helps build trust. (Jackson, a financial professional, in partnership for 2 years and 3 months)

> To pay for major expenses and others, i.e., gas, electricity, etc. It also strengthens our commitment to each other. (James, an administrator, in partnership for 19 years)

> I felt it would demonstrate my commitment to a permanent relationship while producing a way to save for the future. (Michael, a medical professional, in partnership for 2 years and 3 months)

The majority of the couples make equal contributions to the joint account. In the case of couples in which partners make unequal contributions to the joint account, there is usually a big income difference between the partners.

## Complete Pooling

This is the least common management style arrangement, adopted by about one-seventh of the sample. Complete pooling in most cases means that the partners do not keep individual accounts. All of their financial resources therefore are put into a joint account to which both the partners have equal access. The joint account was opened between one to seven years into their partnerships. Except one, all of the couples in this case are cohabiting, which probably indicates that living together facilitates such an arrangement.

The primary motivation behind this management style appears to be the couples' perception that a joint account is a symbol of commitment and a consequence of sharing their lives together, alongside practical convenience. The experience of James and Nigel typifies this. They have been together for 3 years and 3 months. They started living together in a jointly-owned apartment when the partnership was about one year old. Both James, an administrator, and Nigel, an engineering professional, earn between £13000 and £16999 annually. Having tried the partial separate management style, they began pooling all of their financial resources during the third year of their partnership. They tell their story below.

> *James*: We tried it in a different way at first when we first started living here. We had the joint account and also separate personal accounts so that we would have control over some of our own money, and do what we wanted with it. But then later we thought, why? What's the problem? Isn't operating three accounts when we could operate with one ridiculous? Is there a problem with operating with one? We listened to what other people said and the way they kept finances. We decided no. We spend money in very similar patterns. Neither of us is an excessive buyer or waster. We decided in the end for the efficiency of that sort of financial management. It makes more sense to have everything shared. In a relationship based on trust, I see no reason not to [have a joint account]. Any large payments made by either of us are discussed previously anyway.

*Nigel*: It became nonsensical to keep separate accounts going once we were living together. We are both earning money on our own, and we are co-owners of our home.

Complete pooling as a symbol of commitment is also clearly illustrated in the experience of Alan and Nigel who have been together for 10 years and 2 months. Alan, a priest in his early 30s, earns between £9000 and £12999 annually. Nigel's annual income as a teacher is also in the same bracket. They now jointly own a car. They were separated primarily because of work commitments, and their intention to live together only materialized when the partnership was 8 years old. They began pooling their financial resources together as soon as they started cohabiting. They explain:

*Alan*: We put all our money into the bank and the building society accounts. We are both signatories on both the accounts. We assume that all our money is joint. It's a natural consequence of sharing life. It's a symbol of commitment and it is so much more convenient.

*Nigel*: Up until two years ago, when we moved in here together, we had separate houses and separate bank accounts. Since I moved in here, we have had a lot more money available and we spend it together. We now regard all income as joint. I suppose because we feel we share everything including money.

Similarly, Calvin, a priest in his late 20s, and Clive, a financial professional in his mid-20s, who have been together for 5 years also put forward the same argument:

*Calvin*: At first, we couldn't be bothered trying to remember whose turn it was to pay. Within months we were past caring whose money it was. It's ours.

*Clive*: We share our belongings as part of our commitment to each other, so a joint account is a natural conclusion to this. We just have one joint account between us and everything goes in and comes out.

It is clear from the views above that a joint account is perceived to be a symbol of commitment, a natural consequence of sharing life together, particularly when it involves cohabitation. There is, however, Paul and Winston, an interesting couple. Paul puts all of his income into Winston's account, and Winston takes complete charge of the financial management. As a result, a joint account proves unnecessary.

Paul, a musician in his late 50s, earns between £5000 and £8999 annually. He gives all of his earnings to his partner of 16 years, whose annual income as a technician is in the £13000-£16999 bracket. They have both drawn up wills which name each other as the main beneficiaries. Paul explains their management style:

> I sometimes earn about two hundred pounds a week and I just give it to him when I come home and he just gives me however much I need. He invests, pays bills. He keeps full accounts of the whole thing. He has total control over the whole thing because he is totally trustworthy and terribly generous. If I say I want a CD, he won't say, "No, you bought one last week," or anything like that. On the other hand, I am not extravagant.

In spite of the fact that a joint account is unnecessary in the case of Paul and Winston, it is clear that, like the other couples in this category, they consider the complete pooling of their financial resources a symbol of their commitment to each other.

## INCOME DIFFERENCE AND EGALITARIANISM

Philip Blumstein and Pepper Schwartz comment that, "even gay male couples gain advantage over one another when one partner has a high income."[4] Is this the case for these couples? Eleven of the 30 couples I interviewed have an income difference between partners of at least £10000 per annum. However, only one of these couples perceive that the income difference has an impact on their decision-making process.

This couple, Jerry and Keith, have been together for 13 years. Jerry is a teacher earning an annual income of between £9000 and £12999 and Keith, a medical professional with an income of between £21000 and £24999. They keep separate individual accounts but hold a joint account to cover household expenses. Jerry contributes only 25 percent to the joint account. He admits that this might have an impact on the decision-making process.

> It started off that way. When I left university and I was living with him, I was unemployed and he was in full-time employment. He had all the money. So it was his house, his money. Obviously he decided what was going to happen with it. I was living in his house and in return for that I was trying to learn how to do housework. So decisions on when and

where to go on holiday, and how much to spend on what, they were in his hands because he had the money. Now his income is twice more than mine. So, the economic imbalance seems to have a knock-on effect into every aspect of the relationship.

Jerry is also 12 years younger than Keith. Jerry admits that the age difference also plays a part in the inegalitarian decision-making process. However, he is not perturbed by it, as he explains further:

I don't feel negative about the fact that he leads and I follow. In fact, being with somebody like Keith who has got the money, experience, and presence, makes me feel really secure. So I like it and I am quite happy not to make too many of my own decisions.

Keith, on the other hand, has this to say about the effects of age and financial differences:

I think there is a tendency for me to lead, being the older one and owning the house. There is a tendency for me to lead. I mean being dominant. But that has never been an issue. Quite often in smaller things he is quite happy to follow and be led. He is quite happy with that.

The story of Jerry and Keith illustrates that income difference can have an impact on the decision-making process within a partnership. The partner with the higher earning power appears to be the more dominant one in decision-making. However, this need not be problematic. In this case, both Jerry and Keith welcome such an arrangement.

Nevertheless, their experience is the exception rather than the rule. For all of the other 10 couples, none perceive that the decision-making process is affected by a huge income difference. This is typified by Paul, a civil servant, and Kieran, an accountant. They have been together for 4 years but they do not live together. Paul earns an annual income between £17000 and £20999, while Kieran earns between £29000 and £32000. They manage their finances independently. Paul contributes about 25 percent to cover joint expenditures. They both agree that this income difference has no effect on the decision-making process of their partnership.

*Paul*: This is a mutual agreement really. I think Kieran on the whole offers to pay more than I do. I mean I try to make up for this by buying something else later on. So I try to contribute my part. I think it is important to say that he does that because he is able to. In the very early days of our relationship, he didn't have as much money as I did. I think at that stage I contributed more than he did. But the situation has changed slightly now. So it depends on what financial resources we each have at the time. We help each other. We don't take advantage of each other in this area.

*Kieran*: I make a greater contribution because I earn more. I don't think that gives me the edge in decision-making. It gives me a sense of comfort in that I know that I can afford it. But I don't think it gives me a form of superiority in the relationship. I think what gives me the edge in decision-making is my professional background. I have been trained to make snap decisions and judgements. Even that I don't think affects the relationship adversely.

Charles and Jimmy are another good example. Charles, an administrator, earns between £9000 and £12999 a year. On the other hand, Jimmy, a senior teacher, has an annual income of between £21000 and £24999. They manage their finances completely separately. When asked if this situation gives him the edge in decision-making, Jimmy says:

No. I feel that the money I have got is ours. I must provide for my partner. The situation at the moment is that his income is very small compared to mine. I don't like to be in the position where when you love someone he has to be an equal in the financial sense. So I'll share it whenever necessary.

It appears that the imbalance in incomes need not adversely affect egalitarianism in the decision-making process within the partnership. In fact, all of the couples report that their current financial arrangements are the result of a joint decision between partners. Income difference has the potential for inegalitarianism, but if both partners are committed to egalitarianism, that potential would not develop into an area of contention.

# CHAPTER 5

# The "S" Factor: Sex

Sex is an explosive topic within our culture. It is often grossly exaggerated and unrealistically presented in the mass media. Gay sexuality is not spared in this case. It has been subjected to a multitude of stereotypes, principally because of the psycho-pathological lens through which it is perceived socially. We often hear comments that gay men are "promiscuous," and that they replicate the active/passive roles in their sexual relations. The truth of the matter is, we soon realize how little we actually know about this topic when we jettison the stereotypes to which we subject ourselves. This chapter aims to enlighten us on this, arguably the most sensitive, dimension of gay male partnerships.

For nine of the 30 couples I interviewed, their sex life within the partnership is non-existent. This, however, does not mean that the sexual dimension of their partnerships is entirely absent. The nonexistence of sex life within the partnership does not preclude the possibility of sexual encounters outside the partnership. I will discuss this issue of sexual exclusivity in the last section. All, except one, of these partnerships are more than 10 years old, with 33 years as the longest. The mean is 18 years and 5 months. Why has sex ceased in these nine partnerships? The scenario can be attributed to three primary factors.

## OLD AGE

Age is a significant factor affecting a person's sex drive and inter-est in sex. The respondents in these partnerships are between the ages of 45 and 75, with a mean age of 56.8 years. To them, ageing adversely affects the desire for sex. When this takes place in tandem with the increase in the length of the partnerships, which increases its stability and significance, partners then shift their focus to other elements of the partnerships rather than sex. In this connection, Philip Blumstein and Pepper Schwartz comment that, "gay men are very oriented to sexual expression in general, but as their relation-ships mature they rely less on sexuality as a focus for their commit-ment." [1]

The ageing effect is typically expressed by John, a priest in his 50s. He has been in a 23-year-old partnership with Paul, also a priest in his early 60s. They stopped love-making 3 years ago. John tells me:

> I don't mind it [the stopping of love-making]. It doesn't affect the relationship adversely. You see, when you get to our stage you are not young. Therefore, the drive is no longer that strong. You reach the point where the companionship, the care, things that you share, these are the things that are im-portant. You have to see things in proportion. I think it would be very frustrating if I yearned for it and I didn't get it. But it just happens that we crept into it and it has never become an issue.

Ricky and Samuel have been together for 27 years and last made love two years ago. This case is particularly interesting as there is a 23-year age gap between them. Samuel, who is in his late 60s, re-lates:

> The trouble is that I am getting older and he is much younger. I can't help feeling that he is not getting enough of it. But it doesn't seem to be bothering him. It is not a source of conflict. He doesn't seem to mind you see. Frankly, our rela-tionship is so good that it doesn't bother me in any way.

On the other hand, Ricky, who is in his mid-40s, acknowledges the adjustment of his attitude in coping with the situation:

> I find it rather difficult to cope with. But I mean one has to. You just know that that particular part is no longer as fresh as it was. So you think about other things, do other things. You get involved in living. I suppose I do get sexually frus-

trated. But I believe in self-control. I believe in setting your mind that this is the situation and it has a lot of good parts to it. Sex is just a small part of the relationship. Samuel is actually near 70. He is not as responsive as before. But the quality of the relationship is not affected. I don't believe in crying about things. I mean that is the situation. One has got to get used to it and get on with life.

The nonexistence of sex within these partnerships does not appear to generate any major conflicts. This is primarily due to the partners' acceptance of the natural inevitability of ageing and the subsequent loss of sexual interest. Attention is shifted to other elements, for instance, trust and emotional attachment, which they have accumulated throughout the partnerships.

In addition, four of the nine partnerships were sexually nonexclusive before the love-making within the partnerships stopped. Therefore, partners who are still interested in sex could fulfill their need outside the partnership, thus reducing the possibility of sexual frustration within the partnership, which can be destabilizing. Kirk, in his 70s, expresses this:

The stopping of sex did adversely affect the relationship at the beginning. But it was counterbalanced by the steady improvement in the intellectual relationship. So it didn't make me want to stop seeing Simon [his partner]. It just made me more firmly resolve to look further for somebody with whom I could have physical sex.

However, the stopping of love-making within the partnership does not necessarily lead to outside sexual encounters. In the case of Ricky and Samuel, whom I have already mentioned, Samuel, the younger partner, does not resort to sexual contacts outside of the partnership owing to his commitment to sexual exclusivity, buttressed by his religious beliefs.

## LOSS OF SEXUAL INTEREST IN PARTNER

Two of the nine couples cite this as the primary reason for the scenario. A similarity between them is that both couples have been sexually nonexclusive since the beginning of their partnerships. James and Tom, who have been together for almost 16 years, started the partnership with an explicit agreement that it would be sexually nonexclusive. This means that they could have outside sexual contacts either separately or together. Sexual nonexclusivity became such a major feature of their partnership that for a period of two to three years they lived together with a third party with whom they were both sexually involved.

Tom, a manager in his late 40s, who initiated the stopping of love-making with James in the eleventh year of their partnership, considers a general loss of interest in sex the primary reason:

> You know, you don't get turned on as you used to be. You know, sex is about excitement. But the excitement decreases after a few years. I found myself coming back from work and fell asleep and not wanting to do anything. It's hard to say. It is just something that creeps up on you. It is less exciting. And I just can't be bothered.

Tom, however, continues to seek outside sexual contacts "on a very occasional basis." James, an architect in his late 40s who also has outside sexual contacts, considers the situation "a source of disappointment but not a source of conflict." He elaborates further:

> Sex isn't there anymore. But all the other things are there. I mean, that's sufficient anyway. I mean if we do not touch each other, that would be intolerable. But we are very physical with each other. I mean, it is surprising what you can do when you are really committed.

The story of Tom and James highlights two salient points. First, the stopping of love-making is not perceived as an indication of the decline of emotional intimacy and love between the partners. Second, having been in a partnership characterized by mutually agreed upon sexual nonexclusivity, both partners meet their sexual needs outside the partnership, thus diminishing sexual frustration.

It appears that the appropriate perception of love-making, emotional intimacy, and sexual nonexclusivity actually helps maintain the stability of the partnership. This highlights an important point. Sexual nonexclusivity must not be viewed negatively under all circumstances. If mutually agreed upon, it can be a means to reduce sexual frustration of partners who have stopped love-making but are still emotionally committed.

Alan, a medical professional, and Jon, a manager, are both in their late 40s. They have been together for 22 years and they stopped love-making in the eleventh year. Jon admits to having lost his interest in Alan, and having outside sexual contacts on a fortnightly basis. He did not permit this section of the interview to be tape-recorded in view of its sensitive nature. However, Alan's response is consistent with Jon's admission:

Jon just basically lost interest in me sexually. I think he was having a much more interesting time with other people. It just stopped being something he was interested in. I was disappointed. <You just accepted that?> Yes. I grew up in a family that disapproved strongly of sex except for having babies. At a personal level, I am actually very shy about discussing sex. I think if there is any problem about it, I would just let the matter drop, which is what happened. I am sure he still has flings outside.

In this case, sexual nonexclusivity on Jon's part appears to be the cause for the eventual stopping of love-making in this partnership. Alan, however, has accepted the reality.

## SEXUAL INCOMPATIBILITY

Different sexual tastes also can adversely affect the sexual attraction between partners. Jackson and Francis, who have been together for 2 years and 3 months, are in this situation. I have told their story at length in Chapter 3. They were, at the point of interview, considering the dissolution of their partnership. This prospect is precipitated by a high degree of incompatibility in many mutually identified areas such as career goals and sex life. Both of them acknowledge the existence of sexual incompatibility:

*Jackson*: I like to be very involved in sex, hug and kiss a lot. To me orgasm is not really an issue. Francis' mind is completely different. So I felt that there is a massive gap there. I would rather have sex with someone I don't know. I like sex to be free.

*Francis*: I'm not particularly wonderful at sex. Jackson is quite excited and enthusiastic about it. When combined with other conflicts in the relationship, we know that we both want different things. There is no need to pretend. We don't. We can't. So we stopped.

Beginning their partnership 2 years and 3 months ago with an explicit agreement of sexual exclusivity, Jackson and Francis agreed to stop their sex life after two years. They then began to explore outside sexual encounters separately. When I interviewed them, they were at the stage of negotiation and construction of ground rules, for instance, whether a third party could be brought home and whether there would be a need to purchase an extra bed for this purpose.

The shift from sexual exclusivity to nonexclusivity is an outcome of their negotiation and redefinition of the boundaries of their partnership, which transcends the sexual dimension. I would reiterate that this couple is an example *par excellence* of the in-built flexibility within a gay partnership which allows the partners to constantly engage themselves in boundary and constitutional negotiation, due to the nonexistence of an explicit social script.

On the whole, only one of the nine couples has remained sexually exclusive since the termination of their sex life within the partnership. The stopping of love-making within the partnership offers one couple the mutually agreed upon opportunity of sexual exploration outside the partnership. The other seven couples were sexually nonexclusive before sex within the partnership stopped.

## THE IMPORTANCE OF SEX

For couples whose sex life within the partnership is still active, they consider sex "important," "vital," or "quite important." However, they qualify that by emphasizing that sex is not the most important aspect of their partnership. James and Nigel, who have been together for 3 years and 3 months, express this point:

> *James*: It is an important part of the relationship. It is a very therapeutic, very bonding experience. It's not the focus of the relationship. It might have been at one time in the early days. But it is not the focus now. It is actually an expression of those things that are focused. Things like companionship, affection, and love that we have for each other. And the natural expression of that is physical intimacy. So it feels good.

> *Nigel*: It's important obviously, because it's the closeness and the way of showing something. But I think more important is the communication and being honest with each other.

Tom, a musician who has been in a partnership for 6 years and 7 months, asserts in the same vein:

> It's not amazingly important, but important. I don't regard sex as the most significant thing in a relationship. But it is satisfying and it is nice, and it makes me feel happy and secure. It's good.

Putting companionship, affection and love before sex, these responses typify those of many others. The positive attitude toward sex is also expressed in theological terms:

I think it is important in theological terms, because we are created physical people. We have bodies and we should celebrate that. I think it is the expression of the ultimate intimacy. So it is only normal that we should have a wonderful, exciting, and fulfilling sex life. (Calvin, late 20s, a priest)

I enjoy it. I think it is sacramental. It is a visible sign of the inward and spiritual grace. To have that ease with another person's body is very important. I think the fact that my body is available to him to touch whenever he wants to is an important foundation for other bits of the relationship. (Michael, late 30s, a priest)

The accounts above reflect that they are at ease with sex within a partnership, even when it is viewed from a religious perspective. This, I would argue, is a result of their positive self-image as gay Christians. In spite of the Church's official position, which is against the expression of the homosexual orientation, they do not view, in a negative light, the physical expression of their sexuality within a relational context. This point will be elaborated on further.

## FREQUENCY OF SEXUAL ACTIVITY

Many gay men make a distinction between *making love* to their partners in the primary partnership and *having sex* with third parties beyond the confines of the partnership.[2] Unlike the former, the latter is carried out without, or with very little, emotional attachment, solely for recreational purposes. In the case of these couples, the former is certainly more appropriate. Therefore, I use this term to refer to the sexual activity within these partnerships.

On the average, a great majority (71.4 percent) of the respondents report that love-making takes place twice a week or less. The highest monthly frequency reported is 24. The lowest monthly frequency is once, reported by both partners of the same partnership. On the other hand, the mean monthly frequency is 7.7, almost twice a week.

The most significant factor affecting this frequency is the length of the partnership. The general assumption arising from past research is that the longer the partnership, the lower the frequency, as familiarity between partners increases and limerence decreases.[3] These couples do not appear to demonstrate this trend conclusively. In fact, the couple who reported the highest average frequency has been together for 14 years. On the other hand, the couple who reported the lowest frequency have been together for 10 years and 2 months. This general assumption, however, appears to apply to most couples.

Paul, a musician in his late 50s, has been in a partnership with Winston for 16 years. He relates:

> The frequency [twice a month] is just about right for me at the moment. I mean once we would tend to make love five times in a weekend. But when somebody is with you all the time, it decreases. Making love is about several more things than just having an orgasm. It is about physical warmth and cuddling and all that. We do that anyway.

What is clear from this account is that there is a shift of perception about sexual activity as the partnership grows. In the initial stage, mutual sexual excitement naturally leads to a high frequency of sexual activity. But as the partnership develops, more mechanisms are developed for the expression of mutual emotional intimacy and love, such as an increased level of mutual tolerance and acceptance. The focus on sex is therefore diffused. However, the point of this transition seems to vary from couple to couple. Ryan, an administrator in a one-year-old partnership, expresses the same sentiment that Paul expressed despite the great difference in length between their respective partnerships:

> It is one of those odd things that as you get more and more into the relationship. When we first met and first started living together, sex was a very very active part of our lives. We would be doing it a couple of times a day, three or four times on the weekends. Gradually, as we became more complacent with each other, now it is sort of a couple of times a week. So when we first met, we spent a lot more time over sex. It was a lot more imaginative and exciting. It's very easy for complacency to creep in. Now sex can be a little bit perfunctory. We are both aware of that and do try to make more time for it.

Moses, a teacher in his mid-30s, also acknowledges the working of this factor in his 15-year-old partnership:

> I guess like any relationships we started off [making love] frequently, then [it] becomes less. I think in a relationship, it's a case of novelty, you know. I mean familiarity and then it is about sort of trying to maintain our relationship. Sex, it's like becoming jaded. That's all.

Admittedly, there are other factors that affect the frequency of sexual activity. Factors such as separate living arrangements and work patterns are to a large extent beyond the control of the couples.

## SATISFACTION WITH SEX LIFE

How satisfied are the respondents with their sex life within the partnerships? I asked each individual respondent of these 21 partnerships to rate on a scale of 1 ("extremely dissatisfied") to 10 ("extremely satisfied") in this connection. Table 3 tells the story.

**Table 3**
**Level of Satisfaction with Sex Life within Partnership**

| Rating | No. of Respondent | Percentage |
|--------|-------------------|------------|
| 1 to 4 | 4 | 9.5 |
| 5 to 6 | 4 | 9.5 |
| 7 to 8 | 24 | 57.2 |
| 9 to 10 | 10 | 23.8 |

N = 42
Mean Rating = 7.2

Table 3 indicates that 80 percent of the respondents give a rating of 7 and above, indicating that they are highly satisfied with their sex life within the partnership. There exists a positive relationship between the level of satisfaction and the frequency of love-making. The level of satisfaction in sex life increases as the average monthly frequency of love-making increases. As the average monthly frequency increases from "between 1 to 4 times," "between 5 and 8 times," and "between 9 and 12 times" to "more than 12 times," the mean ratings increase from 6.2 to 7.7, 8.0 and 8.2. Thus, the higher the average frequency of love-making, the higher the respondent's level of satisfaction with his sex life.[4]

An interesting observation can be made when the level of satisfaction is related to living arrangement: cohabiting respondents have a *higher* average frequency of love-making but a *lower* level of satisfaction compared to their noncohabiting counterparts. The mean rating for the former is 6.9, against the latter's 7.7. This means that the constant availability of a sexual partner within the partnership understandably results in a higher frequency of love-making but not a higher level of satisfaction. This is probably because the limited availability of the partner for non-cohabiting respondents heightens their appreciation of the opportunity for the physical expression of their emotional attachment and intimacy. Cohabiting respondents, on the other hand, might engage in love-making because of the mere fact that the partner is available. Love-making, in this case, can become perfunctory.

## ROLE-TAKING IN LOVE-MAKING

The analysis of sexual activity between gay men has been beset with the concern for the active-passive dichotomy. The "active" partner is assumed to perform, and therefore dominates; and the "passive" partner is assumed to receive, and therefore subordinates. This is done primarily to assess if gay couples replicate what is by and large considered "the conventional heterosexual model" with one partner (usually the male) initiating and performing while the other partner (usually the female) receives. The popular assumption is that gay couples demonstrate "role complementarity," adopting masculine (active/dominant) and feminine (passive/subordinate) roles.[5]

This assumption has inaccurately led to the heavy focus placed on *certain* types of sexual techniques instead of the wide repertoire that gay men explore and practice. Therefore, anal sex and oral sex, which generally fit into the "insertive-receptive" dichotomy, have been conveniently and almost exclusively used as the sexual techniques for the consideration of the "active-passive" model. However, research evidence suggests that the majority of gay men tend to interchange insertive and receptive roles in oral and anal sexual activities.[6]

Besides, we must be cautious not to imply that a partner who has experienced insertive oral or anal sex is the "active" or "dominant" partner while the partner who has experienced receptive oral or anal sex is the "passive" or "subordinate" one. Joseph Harry warned way back in the 1970s that "the concepts of inserter and insertee are not polar opposites... there is a dimension of oral preference among gay males that is independent of active-passive orientations."[7]

Gay male sexuality is much more complex than what the limiting "active-passive" model exemplifies. In the case of oral sex, for instance, a partner who "actively initiates" oral sex might "passively receive" it from his partner. Thus, he is "active" as the role of the initiator and "passive" in the role of the receiver. On the other hand, a partner might on his own initiative perform oral sex on his partner. He is "active" in the initiation of it, although he appears to be "passive" in the execution of the sexual act.[8]

First and foremost, let the 21 couples tell us what they actually do in bed. I asked each individual respondent to fill out during the interview a self-completion questionnaire eliciting information about the different types of sexual techniques they employ in their love-making sessions. Table 4 tells the story.

**Table 4**
**Types of Sexual Techniques and their Frequency of Employment** [9]

| Sexual Technique | Often | Sometimes | Rarely | Never/Tried Few Times |
|---|---|---|---|---|
| Masturbation: | | | | |
| Performing on | | | | |
| Partner | 4 (9.6%) | 8 (19.0%) | 18 (42.9%) | 12 (28.5%) |
| Receiving | 6 (14.3%) | 7 (16.6%) | 19 (45.3%) | 10 (23.8%) |
| Mutual | 19 (45.2%) | 17 (40.5%) | 4 (9.5%) | 2 (4.8%) |
| Fellatio/Oral Sex | | | | |
| Performing | 19 (45.2%) | 17 (40.6%) | 3 (7.1%) | 3 (7.1%) |
| Receiving | 22 (52.4%) | 11 (26.2%) | 9 (21.4%) | 0 (0.0%) |
| Rimming/Oral-anal Contact | | | | |
| Performing | 4 (9.6%) | 7 (16.6%) | 13 (30.9%) | 18 (42.9%) |
| Receiving | 2 (4.8%) | 10 (23.8%) | 13 (30.9%) | 17 (40.5%) |
| Fucking/Penetrative Anal Sex | | | | |
| Performing | 6 (14.3%) | 6 (14.3%) | 18 (42.9%) | 12 (28.5%) |
| Receiving | 4 (9.6%) | 10 (23.8%) | 14 (33.3%) | 14 (33.3%) |
| Body Rubbing/ Friction | | | | |
| Mutual | 20 (47.6%) | 12 (28.6%) | 5 (11.9%) | 5 (11.9%) |
| Other (S&M, Water Sports, Douching, Bondage, Fingering, Scatting, Fisting etc.) | | | | |
| Performing | 0 (0.0%) | 2 (4.8%) | 8 (19.0%) | 32 (76.2%) |
| Receiving | 1 (2.4%) | 0 (0.0%) | 9 (21.4%) | 32 (76.2%) |

Table 4 indicates that the ten most frequently employed sexual techniques are:
1. receptive oral sex
2. mutual body-rubbing/friction
3. (a) insertive oral sex; (b) mutual masturbation
5. (a) receptive masturbation; (b) insertive anal sex
7. (a) performing masturbation on partner; (b) performing rimming; (c) receptive anal sex
10. receiving rimming

It is indeed telling to observe that the experiences of these couples debunk the general assumption that gay men are exceedingly interested in penetrative anal sex (especially insertive). In order of frequency, insertive anal sex is ranked fifth while receptive anal sex is jointly ranked seventh, the second to last on the list. This is evidence that the assumption is more stereotype than truth.

Almost all of the respondents argue that their sexual activities demonstrate a high degree of role exchangeability, depending on, for instance, personal preference. They do not appear to conform to the limiting "active-passive" dichotomy. The following comments are typical.

> Everything we do we take turns when it takes place. Also, sometimes it depends on who is tired and who isn't. There is no fixed kind of role that we play while having sex. So in general in our love-making there is no dominant partner or submissive partner. (Calvin, a priest in his late 20s)

> Not one or the other really. It does vary. There are no fixed roles. I think it very much responds to needs you know. Sometimes I might feel the need to be passive and sometimes it is active. So nothing is set. (James, a civil servant in his late 30s)

> I would tend to be the active partner in terms of anal intercourse because I like it. It is very rare for me to be the passive one. But he is more active in other techniques. It is all sort of equal. (Ryan, an administrator in his mid-30s)

> I think that sex between two men is not active or passive. It is much more equal because you are initiating activities and responding to activities all the time. Even in what appears to be an active-passive dichotomy, the passive partner is in fact much more active than people imagine. It is not grin your teeth and think of England. You are actively involved in what is going on. So I don't like the expression active and passive in the roles of sexual activities because you aren't. All that we do we are both involved in it. (Michael, a priest in his late 30s)

These stories establish the fact that gay men prefer and practice a high degree of role exchangeability in their love-making.[10] There is no role specialization in this respect, as Joseph Harry argues, "participation in gay sexual activities encourages sexual flexibility rather than the sexual role specialization that psychoanalytic or popular conceptions would have us believe."[11]

## CHRISTIANITY AND SEX

Many consider Christianity rather ill-informed about issues related to sex and sexuality. Therefore, it is not surprising to observe that the majority of respondents demonstrate a lack of confidence in the Church on its teaching on sex and sexuality in general, and homosexuality in particular.

Most respondents argue that there is a need to negotiate their private sex life without referring to the Church's conventional teaching:

Christianity itself is muddled about the body. Its teachings on the body tend to be absurd, and worse than absurd. Christian teaching about the body is that it's evil, [which is] extremely misguided. So it would never actually occur to me to take my Christianity into bed. (Simon, an administrator in his late 30s)

Whatever two people want to do together in bed is entirely up to them. If it enhances their love and enjoyment of each other, then fine. I personally would not do anything that would involve physical hurt or pain. But I respect the fact that some people do and it is entirely up to them. (Ryan, an administrator in his mid-30s)

On the whole, the respondents' sexual attitudes reveal that they do adhere to certain principles. While some claim that these principles originate from general human values, some attribute them to Christian norms:

I think that the area in which Christian values come into play is when sex becomes predatory, selfish, exploitative. There should be no manipulation, of using people. That's wrong. It's more like lust, isn't it? Doing rape with consent. When sex is created it is mutual. (Aaron, priest, mid-30s)

We must have a theology of relationships rather than physical act. When people are making love, they should be so spontaneous. They don't think oh we can do this, we can't do that. If it is going to be dangerous then it shouldn't be done. Or if one person wants something and the other person doesn't want it, then it shouldn't be done because this is against his will. (Paul, musician, late 50s)

The above views reveal the similarity between their sexual attitudes with the Christian norms of justice and love. These views

greatly emphasize norms such as free will, respect, relativity, mutu-
ality, and egalitarianism. Marvin Ellison calls this "ethic of common
decency." [12]

In terms of sexual techniques, the majority report that as long as
they are employed within the context of a loving relationship for mutual satisfaction, they should be free to explore and experiment:

> There are still Christians around who say that wherever oral
> sex is found, demons are not far away! But there is abso-
> lutely no limit, no restriction on what we do together, apart
> from what we both enjoy. You discover when you do it. It's
> not evil. It's just love. That's what you discover. It's just love.
> It feels like love. You know it is love and you are giving it as
> love and you receive it as love. And there is no evil in love.
> (Calvin, priest, late 20s)

> I think in the context of a relationship, it's the relationship
> that is Christian. So expressing it [sex] comes naturally. I
> suppose in the context of a relationship, whatever both part-
> ners would be willing to do is all right. I remember someone
> saying that God is far more concerned with what you do with
> your wealth than what you do with your willy. (Michael,
> priest, late 30s)

The respondents' sexual attitudes towards sex and sexual techniques reflect general Christian norms of justice and love. Although
some attribute that to humanistic values rather than Christian,
some specifically acknowledge the influence of Christianity in this
connection. It is quite clear that many reject the institutionalized
Church as their moral arbiter in this respect. However, their sexual
attitudes do manifest broad Christian values. We will explore this
issue further in Chapter 6.


## SEXUAL NONEXCLUSIVITY: BLESSING OR BANE?

Sexual exclusivity is one of the thorniest issues that gay male
couples have to grapple with, and its outcome has a significant impact on the continuity of the partnership itself.[13] Research evidence
suggests that the majority of gay male couples are in sexually nonexclusive or open partnerships. For example, Philip Blumstein and
Pepper Schwartz report that two-thirds of the 1365 gay men they
studied are in open partnerships.[14]

Nevertheless, we should not assume that all gay male couples
begin their partnerships with the cultural ideal that they should be
sexually exclusive. In actuality, many gay male couples begin their

partnerships with either an explicit agreement or implicit understanding about this issue. We need to take into consideration both the expectation and the actual behavior of the couple while examining this issue.[15]

Almost one-third of the couples I interviewed began their partnerships with the expectation that they should be sexually exclusive, and their behavior thus far has been consistent with that. On the other hand, almost one-half of the couples expect their partnerships to be sexually nonexclusive, and their behavior is consistent with the expectation. However, 8 couples expect their partnerships to be sexually exclusive, but are behaviorally nonexclusive. They, failing to be consistent in terms of expectation and behavior, have to develop various strategies to manage the disjunction.

### Commitment to Sexual Exclusivity

Given that male sex role socialization encourages sexual variety, facilitated by the high availability of casual and anonymous sex in the gay male scene, why do some couples negotiate an explicit agreement or implicit understanding that their partnerships should be sexually exclusive, and have managed to live up to that expectation?

Ricky and Samuel, both retirees, have been together for 27 years. They hold undivided commitment to sexual exclusivity:

*Samuel*: I wouldn't want an open relationship. It is just not for me. I would probably say that it is very hard. If you have sex with lots and lots of people, you are giving away little bits of yourself. So there is nothing left. But with another person in a monogamous relationship, you are giving and receiving. You are strengthening yourself.

*Ricky*: I think it is a good thing to have exclusivity. I think it is a good thing to aim and try to achieve. I think lots of things can go wrong if you are not faithful to each other. I don't think the relationship would last. I know that sometimes it is difficult but it is something to work for, I think.

Ricky and Samuel clearly equate exclusivity to fidelity and faithfulness. Sexual exclusivity is therefore a symbol of total commitment and trust to each other. Ryan and Nick, both in their 30s, have been together for one year. They also demonstrate this commitment:

*Ryan*: I believe that in a relationship, one should always be aiming for it being a monogamous relationship, because a re-

lationship is based on physical love and trust. If you regard
sexual activity as being the expression of your love and commitment to another person, then clearly it [sexual nonexclu-
sivity] demeans that trust you specially have for your partner.

*Nick*: I think it is really important. I think it is the notion of
the relationship, the notion of equality. I think that if he or I
felt the need to look elsewhere for sexual gratification, it
wouldn't be just pure sex. I think that is dangerous you
know. I think that is the sign that there are cracks in our relationship or our way of communicating or our emotional relationship, that we need to look elsewhere for gratification. I do
think it is very important.

Some couples explicitly state that their commitment to sexual
exclusivity stems from their commitment to conventional Christian
sexual ethics. They are of the opinion that Christian ideals of monog-
amy, which are equated with faithfulness and fidelity, should be the
moral guidelines for the formation of Christian partnerships. This
applies to both same-sex or cross-sex partnerships. Robert, a priest
whose partnership is 16 years and 6 months old, argues this point
rather eloquently:

For Christians you really should stick with one partner. And I
believe that quite strongly. Because I don't think there is any
other theological model for a sexual relationship that works
in Christian terms. You can't make it fit what I think as the
insides of scripture and tradition about what a sexual relationship is. I think faithfulness to one person actually is quite
a profound thing. I don't think it is just a social convention.
It's something that affects who we are and the people we
grow into. It has something to do with the fact that we are
made in God's image and that we are capable of faithfulness.

In the same vein, Paul, whose partnership is 6 years and 7 months
old, also argues:

Christianity has something to do with this [his commitment].
It has to do with valuing the other person. There is an element of self-sacrifice for the other person, of saying there is
every aspect of our relationship, it is not just about personal
satisfaction. It is about what we can give to one another.
That's what love is about. It's about putting another person
first. Regarding sex as just about having fun and enjoying
yourself actually removes the possibility of sex being about
something that you give. It makes it something you take.

These eloquent arguments are supported by Calvin and Clive. They are both in their 20s and have been together for 5 years. They assert:

> *Calvin*: We are absolutely committed to each other and being faithful to each other and not having any other sexual partners. Initially for me it would be derived from Christianity. It is now tested and proved by experience. I am simply quite confident that partnerships where people are faithful to each other and trust each other are healthy.

> *Clive*: I think there is such a great scope for being hurt if you don't [make the partnership exclusive]. Obviously this is sort of an issue of Christian morals. I feel it is generally not very good to have multiple partners. It can be quite damaging. I certainly feel that would be very damaging to me to have multiple partners.

### Commitment to Sexual Nonexclusivity

Couples who are committed to sexual nonexclusivity typically hold an explicit agreement or implicit understanding about it either at the beginning or at certain point of their partnerships. Inasmuch as agreement has been established at the outset, the actual experiences of sexual nonexclusivity are therefore not viewed as "infidelity" or "unfaithfulness".

In general, they draw a clear line of demarcation between *making love* with their primary partners and *having sex* with casual or anonymous partners, as I have mentioned earlier. This distinction is clearly expressed below:

> It [sexual exclusivity] didn't detract us from the fact that, you know, I love Ian [his partner]. It wasn't a case that I stopped loving him for somebody else. I think that is an important difference. I think being unfaithful is when you sort of want to love somebody else. I think that's what unfaithful means. I think having sex with somebody else isn't quite the same as being unfaithful. (Angus, actor, in a 12-year-old partnership)

Why sexual nonexclusivity? The opportunity for sexual variety and excitement appears to be the primary reason.[16] The following arguments illustrate this point.

> I am very faithful. But I mean in the sense it is complete faithfulness, but it incorporates sleeping with other people. But I am very faithful to him in all the things that matter. I

don't think sex matters to a very great extent. It's something that's done for pleasure. Or it can be part of deepening the relationship. Having sex outside is not a need, it's an occasional pleasure. (Simon, late 20s, in a 14-year-old partnership)

Well sometimes when we sort of have had enough of each other I think it [having outside sexual encounters] is always enriching. We know these things happen and it's neither good nor bad. Obviously, I mean what I would be most anxious about is if he felt or I felt that there was a direct link between the lack of sex between us and our having sex elsewhere... that would bother me and I would do something about it. I like it [having sex outside partnership]. I want it. It's nothing higher or lower than that. (Warren, mid-30s, in a 13-year-old partnership)

Many respondents consider the absence of normative guidelines one of the advantages of being in a gay male partnership. There is a substantial amount of freedom and flexibility for negotiation between partners. Therefore, if both partners agree to have a nonexclusive partnership, that should be the arrangement they develop, instead of uncritically conforming to what they consider the "heterosexual marriage" model. James, an architect in his late 40s, is in a 16-year-old partnership. He argues:

The reason for sexual nonexclusivity is that we don't conform to marriage. Well, they [heterosexual couples] have sex with other people but it is more difficult because they have got children, social conventions and so on. Whereas with us the Church for instance has never recognized the relationship. So what the hell? And so on the whole sexuality seems much more liberal for us. But there are relationships that are monogamous. But I find it hard to believe. It is very rare I think.

Relatedly, some respondents also argue that partners should empower each other to utilize the freedom and flexibility embedded in gay partnerships. It is a symbol of egalitarianism and it helps avoid the possessiveness between partners.

I don't agree in general with sexual exclusivity. I think that partners should trust each other more and allow each other to have whatever sex they feel they need outside the relationship without actually damaging the relationship. With me and Simon [his partner], I don't feel that there would be any risk of the partnership breaking up. So he puts up with any sexual relationships that I may have outside. He doesn't mind. He knows perfectly well that our relationship is secure. (Kirk, whose partnership is 11 years and 7 months old)

It's part of trust. It's so important not to cling onto someone in a relationship. Not trying to control their thoughts nor their body. I don't know about you, but if I feel anyone is trying to cling onto me, my immediate reaction is to pull myself away. So, I think in relationship you give the person the freedom to go away or to come towards you. And that's the sort of freedom which I hope I am giving Warren [his partner]. And this is the sort of freedom I expect from him. I don't want to be hung on to. (Aaron, mid-30s, in a 13-year-old partnership)

Couples who are committed to sexual nonexclusivity tend to reject categorically the conventional Christian sexual ethics upheld by those who are committed to sexual exclusivity. They invariably consider these ethics applicable only to heterosexual partnerships (i.e., marriage). Thus, they are inclined to jettison this "heterosexual model" and construct their own. Moses, a teacher in his mid-30s, asserts:

I think one of the things that I constantly re-evaluate is, whether our relationship is just aping a heterosexual married couple. Because I think the Church has kind of excluded us on paper. There is no official marriage ceremony or anything like that. I think therefore we've got a licence to do whatever we feel. I think we should make our own rule. I think what we actually do is what we are happy with, what we want to do. It's what we consider to be appropriate, or certainly what I consider to be appropriate.

The rejection of conventional Christian sexual ethics is unequivocal. These respondents are more inclined to organize their sexual lifestyles on the basis of their own sense of morality, which might be broadly derived from Christian principles such as love and responsibility. The specific emphasis on exclusivity and its equation to fidelity are, however, rejected. The following arguments offer a glimpse of such an attitude.

I suppose Paul talked about the body being the temple of God and actually treating your body in that sort of way. But I don't think that necessarily means that you are exclusive. I guess it has to do with what is going on between that kind of encounter and how it relates to others and whether there is abuse. I can't see what Christianity can say, because it doesn't say anything, does it? But I think it does in the sense that I follow it from the point of view of responsibility. I respect even people you meet in the cottage [public toilet], you know, that they are human beings. So from that point of view, yes. But otherwise no because it has got nothing to say. The relationship is something that it doesn't support. (James, architect, late 40s)

What one should do is, always be loving and caring and non-exploitative. There can certainly be affection and gentleness. There can be an exchange of pleasure. All of which are very good things. I won't exploit, but a mutual sharing, typically wanting to go to bed and wanting to have fun and enjoy each other. Oh yes! That's almost gospel! [The gospel] doesn't quite say it but I mean I think that is a very Christian thing to do actually. It depends on if for that person it's a very rejoicing thing to do. (John, musician, late 40s)

The accounts above demonstrate that, despite their categorical rejection of conventional Christian sexual ethics, they still adhere to what they perceive as values broadly based on Christian principles.

### Managing the Disjunction between Expectation and Behavior

Less than one-third of the couples I interviewed began their partnerships with the expectation of sexual exclusivity. However, either one or both partners violates that expectation at a certain point of their partnership. What brings about the change? How do they cope with the disjunction between initial expectation and behavior?

Nonexclusivity became a feature of these partnerships within 6 months to 2 years of their inception. Most tell me that outside sexual encounters take place unexpectedly. Having experienced it and realized that it does not necessarily lead to relationship breakdown, they are encouraged to continue. This of course precipitates a reevaluation of their initial expectation. The experience of Jerry, a teacher in a 13-year-old partnership, typifies this progression:

It has developed. When I was first with Keith [his partner], I was very anxious to have a kind of marriage, to be completely exclusive with him. But not long into the relationship I was led astray by someone. I was very upset. I told him about it. He was okay about it. And then I had to begin to think about being realistic about it. Gradually I came to a feeling that I was not the sort of person who would be essentially exclusive naturally. It is simply not practical. I mean it has never bothered him if I have secondary relationships. That means that I could have them and it doesn't bother me or worry me anymore.

The positive response from Keith leads Jerry into a process of reevaluation. Keith, at a later stage, also begins to have outside sexual encounters, albeit with a lower degree of activeness. From this stage on, the expectation of sexual exclusivity changes.

On the other hand, Richard and George, whose partnership is 8 years old, were expectationally and behaviorally exclusive during the first two years of their partnership. However, the desire to experiment sexually beyond the partnership leads to nonexclusivity, as both partners report:

*Richard*: It was me who introduced that. Probably for a couple of years when we started it was very exclusively just us. But because I have always been apparently very interested in cottaging [having anonymous sex in public toilets] and so on, I sort of introduced George to going into places like that and then going to sauna and going to Amsterdam for holiday and so on. So it was really me who started it all, although George obviously participated and appeared to be participating quite keenly and equally. But it did come from me after about a couple of years into the relationship.

*George*: As far as I was concerned, it wasn't going to develop to that [nonexclusivity]. It was just Richard and me. It was probably like that for two years. We had a little discussion every now and then about whether we should broaden our horizons a bit, like start doing cottaging or going back to somebody else's flat or whatever. So it was like Richard experimenting and me going along with it.

*Regulatory Mechanisms*

Couples develop different regulatory mechanisms to manage their nonexclusive lifestyles in order to prevent the destabilization of their primary partnerships. Therefore, they can experience the security of a primary partnership and having the opportunity to seek sexual gratification outside. Most establish ground rules to construct the framework within which outside sexual encounters are considered acceptable to each partner.

I am sure Jon [his partner] still has flings outside. <Are you upset about that?> No, not really. I would feel upset if he were with somebody in the house when I came home. He sees

others outside or when I am away. That I don't mind. We
have a sort of house rule. People don't come back if the other
one is here because it is not very nice. (Alan, medical professional, late 40s)

The ground rule for Alan and Jon is clear: no casual sex partners
are to be brought home if the other partner is present. This is for the
obvious reason of minimizing embarrassment and the possibility of
jealousy.

For Richard and George, whom I have mentioned just now, the
ground rule is the opposite. Casual sex partners can only be brought
home if the other partner is also present. Richard spells this out
clearly:

We had an arrangement, that we would not bring someone
back here as individuals. But if we saw someone that we
thought might be attracted to the other one, then we will
have a threesome here. Or if we went out cottaging on weekends together or whatever we would have a threesome. So it
was either limited sex in public toilets or whatever or it was
a threesome together. And that was the arrangement that no
one was going to be brought back here without the other person being here. We wouldn't bring someone home, it would be
by arrangement. So it wouldn't be done until it was discussed
or arranged between the two of us. So this is what we were
planning to do as a couple.

It is clear that the ground rule that casual sex partners can only
be brought home if the other partner is also present is for the purpose of engaging in threesomes. This ensures the participation of
both partners, and in return minimizes the possibility of a sense of
exclusion and jealousy.

The compliance to the mutually agreed upon ground rules is a
sign of trust between partners. The violation of the ground rule is
therefore perceived as the betrayal of that trust. It also reinforces
that their primary partnerships are special and uncompromised by
outside sexual encounters.

Some respondents choose to conceal information about outside
sexual encounters, realizing that such information would prove dis-
tressing to their partners. The concealment aims to minimize the
possibility of jealousy and a sense of insecurity. This is especially
true in the case of Cliff and Michael. Cliff, a priest, regularly has outside sexual encounters while Michael, a medical professional, does
not. Michael is in general accepting of Cliff's behavior because of his
confidence in the stability of the partnership, but he insists that he
does not want to know about Cliff's outside sexual encounters.

I don't think it [sexual nonexclusivity] would bother me because I know that there is no way that he would leave me for anybody else. If sex happens, it's sex. It's not a threat to me. There is nobody that can be a threat to me. I don't feel threatened at all. If he should have a sexual relationship with somebody else, it wouldn't bother me. Although I am not sure I necessarily want to hear the details of it.

Realizing Michael's position in this respect, Cliff resorts to concealing all of the information about his outside sexual encounters. In stark contrast to Michael and Cliff, some couples mutually agree to disclose freely between themselves information about outside sexual encounters. This policy of honesty is to minimize a sense of exclusion a partner might feel in response to his partner's encounters. In this case, fidelity means honesty rather than exclusivity.

Mutually disclosing information about outside sexual encounters also indicates the equality they uphold in their partnership. Paul, a civil servant in his late 20s, explains, "Because he has done something similar [having outside sexual encounters] and told me. So it balances each other and so it doesn't create a problem for us."

Some also greatly emphasize the prevention of the possible development of a casual sexual encounter or "fling" into an ongoing affair. Charles, a manager in his mid-20s, explains:

You see a fling is purely lust. I can tolerate that. But I probably couldn't tolerate if it were lust and emotional. I think relationship is about two things, sexuality and the emotional side.

This distinction is important in order that one does not compromise the primacy and significance of one's partnership with casual sexual encounters. Jerry, a teacher in his early 30s, argues:

I do not give these things [outside sexual encounters] a time commitment. If I am involved with somebody, that person has to take the windows in my dairy. I do not take time to give to somebody under these circumstances.

On the whole, we can see that couples develop different regulatory mechanisms to manage their nonexclusive lifestyles. The effective management of these mechanisms minimizes the negative impact it might exert on the partnership. One of the most widely used mechanism is the establishment of ground rules. It is the violation of such ground rules that threatens the stability of the partnership and not the actual outside sexual encounter itself.

**The Impacts of Change: Two Examples**

The change of sexual arrangement involves the handling of a very sensitive issue of the partnership. Some couples explicitly negotiate the possibility to change their initial expectation of sexual nonexclusivity. However, to most couples, the negotiation only takes place after one or both partners have had an outside sexual encounter. This negotiation signifies the   process of "relationship remodeling," through which the relationship adapts in order to ensure its continuity and enhance its quality.[17] Here, I will tell the stories of two couples to illustrate the impact such a change can effect.

I have already mentioned above about Richard and George, whose partnership is 8 years old. They explicitly agreed on sexual exclusivity at the beginning of their partnership. However, their desire for sexual variety and experimentation leads to their turning to non-exclusivity after two years. The nonexclusive lifestyle persisted for almost six years until an experience that almost resulted in the dissolution of their partnership. They are now determined to adopt an exclusive life-style.

I must mention that what led to the virtual dissolution of the partnership was not sexual nonexclusivity itself, which functioned well until this crisis, but the *violation of the ground rule* that they have explicitly established: that no partner should engage in a casual sexual encounter at home in the absence of the other.

This couple, as I have discussed before, was experiencing a great relationship breakdown owing to the inegalitarian decision-making in their partnership that breeds overdependence and domination (see Chapter 3). Being dissatisfied with it and being tired of the sexual experimentation, George turned to a casual sexual partner for affection and brought him home in Richard's absence, thus deliberately excluding him from the ongoing affair. When he was caught red-handed by Richard, the result was disastrous. Both of them acknowledge this:

> *George*: I had a relationship with someone and I didn't want Richard to know that, which is totally detrimental to everything we have ever done or stood for before.

> *Richard*: And that's quite devastating because that goes against the utter trust that I had in him. I dislike the idea of having been misled.

The massive process of reevaluation leads this couple out of the possibility of dissolution. Both are now determined to revert to sexual exclusivity to completely eradicate the possibility of another crisis of such a nature again, as Richard relates:

The biggest change is that we have frequently indulged in threesomes together with other people. But we will not do that now. We have committed ourselves to the relationship in terms of not involving anyone else sexually in the relationship, which is a complete change from what we have done before. So you know it's an exclusive relationship just to us and we won't look for other people to come in. Now we are really interested in the quality of our relationship rather than the quantity of sex that involves other people.

Their experience confirms the point I made earlier, that sexual nonexclusivity is not on its own problematic to certain couples. What generates conflict is the violation of the ground rules they have established. The three stages this couple goes through, from sexual exclusivity to nonexclusivity and back to exclusivity, also signifies the flexibility a gay partnership has in constantly adapting to various circumstances. Of course, such a process has the potential to lead the partnership to dissolution as much as to a better-adjusted state.

Conflicting expectations between partners on the issue of sexual exclusivity can have far-reaching implications on the partnership. This is the case for Simon and John, who have been together for 14 years. John entered the partnership with the expectation that it should be completely exclusive, contradictory to Simon's. When John discovered Simon's outside sexual encounters, he perceived that as a sign of relationship breakdown. They tell me their story and the pain involved.

*Simon*: I think John has assumed that sexually it would be a monogamous relationship. I think that's his assumption and certainly what he wanted. But it wasn't my assumption that it would be. I think he was very hurt. But at the end he overcame his hurt. I think a lot of it was when he realized that the relationship wasn't under threat and there was no threat in these little sexual encounters, I think the problem seemed to evaporate. But I think when I found out he was getting very hurt about it, I knew I did it at the wrong time. So I knew I should stop for a while.

*John*: It [the partnership] was very new then. So the first couple of years were very difficult for me because Simon had been much more into the gay scene than I was. The idea of what now called the recreational sex, he understood and I didn't understand it. It was silly really, because of my stupid idea about, you know, you had to have somebody for yourself and that was it. It's very "jealousing." I suppose it's just part of being immature. So there were conflicts about that. I think

I upset him that I didn't understand. But I think there is
nothing worse than sexual jealousy. I mean he accepted that
our relationship was the most important thing for him.... So I
suppose I experimented a bit more and then found that it
was quite enjoyable. I think I became more secure with myself, and I accepted myself fully. I suppose it took me years
and years. It must have dawned on me one day that Simon
was completely trustworthy and reliable, that nothing bad
was going to happen. And I suppose I feel loved and cher-
ished and wanted and needed. [Outside sexual encounters]
became insignificant. So someone spends half-an-hour with
somebody else, so what? I just hope he had a good time. The
only thing that would upset me was, if he ceased to love me
and decided the relationship wasn't worth carrying on with.
That would be devastating.

John's long account reveals his initial perception of sexual nonexclusivity as a sign of relationship breakdown and a threat to the
partnership itself. His subsequent change of attitude reflects the in-
creasing confidence he has in the solid foundation of the partnership.
Both partners are now sexually nonexclusive, and occasionally participate in threesomes.

The experience of John and Simon supports David Blasband's
and Letitia Peplau's argument that, "gay male couples experiment
with and modify sexual agreement as their needs or circumstances
change." [18] More broadly, this is an example of how gay male couples
often use a trial-and-error approach to construct relationship rules,
due to the lack of structural and cultural guidelines available to
them. [19]

## CHAPTER 6

# Spirituality and Sexuality: Managing a Christian Faith

Being gay and Christian? Many would consider these two aspects a contradiction in terms. At the early stage of my research, one of the questions most frequently asked of me was, "Can being gay be compatible with being Christian?" In this chapter, I will continue the stories by presenting gay Christians who can confidently answer that question with an unequivocal YES! The focus, however, is not on the individual respondents' journeys of sexuality. I want to focus on the present, not the past.[1] Here, I will concentrate primarily on the couples as a whole, in order to illustrate how they manage a Christian faith that incorporates their spirituality and sexuality.

### THE PAIN

Discovering one's homosexuality is a daunting experience to say the least. Many gay Christians, having internalized the conventional Church teachings that are negative toward homosexuality, experience a great deal of guilt and shame. This form of internalized homophobia is debilitating and painful. It has a profound negative impact on their self-image and social adjustment.[2]

Thankfully, human courage often prevails in the face of such a brazen challenge. The gay male Christians I interviewed are testimony to that. They have come a very long way in their respective journeys of sexuality. Even though they now are being in committed and fulfilling partnerships, they can still recall the pain of coming to terms with their sexuality and spirituality in the initial stages of their journeys. Guilt and shame were inescapable feelings to them, clearly expressed in the typical account below:

> There was a strong struggle trying to cope with my Christian-
> ity and sexuality. When I first came out to myself, I came out
> within myself and Christ. And a lot of my prayers were re-
> lated to conversations very much about my sexuality, because
> I was angry that I was gay. (Jimmy, a Baptist in his mid-
> 30s)

Moses, an Anglican in his mid-30s, had his first sexual experience with a member of the same sex at the age of ten, although he
did not label the encounter as "homosexual." He tells me about the
pain he has endured:

> I never realized seriously that anything was "wrong" until I
> sort of went to secondary school. I mean in the third year of
> primary school I had quite a long-term, you know, sexual re-
> lationship with two boys. And I just thought everybody was
> doing such things. I mean I knew it was wrong to tell your
> parents. I think adolescence was really difficult. Between the
> ages of 16 and 19, I think I went through a phase of actually,
> you know, making up some elaborate lies, you know, to cover
> up the real me. I went through psychiatric problems which
> caused temporary paralysis. I couldn't walk. I had strange
> pain, and I went through all sorts of medical checks and
> things like that, and then I ended up with a psychologist.
> You know, the thing I learned from that is that I was living
> this double existence: the real me and then the me who was
> trying to be a school teacher. I think, you know, I had great
> fear that my peers and students would find out. So following
> that after a long time, I sort of opened up and led a much
> healthier lifestyle.

Moses' story about the difficulty in reconciling his sexuality and
Christianity speaks for many. Of course, not everyone ends up on the
psychiatrist's couch, but the pain is undeniably immense. However,
they seem to have come a very long way and developed a positive
self-image, despite the continued lack of support from the Church.


## THE VICTORY

That these gay Christians continue to look for ways to cope with
the seeming incompatibility between their sexuality and spirituality
is a story of human courage and resilience. An invariable response to

the initial guilt and shame is to look for an answer surreptitiously. This itself is a long journey of alienating reflexivity. Unfortunately, many gay Christians stay in this stage for the rest of their lives. Some, however, manage to break this chain of self-alienation and claim the victory.[3] Moses, for instance, has now developed a positive self-image despite the immense difficulty he experienced. When asked if he regrets being gay now, he tells me:

> No. I like being gay. I don't want to be straight. God, it would ruin my life! I wouldn't be with Ron [his partner] in the same way.

Charles, a Roman Catholic in his mid-20s, speaks for many when he responds to the same question:

> No. I don't regret being gay at all. I am very happy being gay. You know, otherwise, I wouldn't go on the Gay Pride March and shout my head off. I am very proud to be gay.

While not all proud gay men participate in the Gay Pride March, Charles' positive self-image is clearly manifested in his account. His happiness about being gay is supported by Simon, an Anglican in his late 30s:

> No. I don't regret being gay at all. Being gay does not make me a less able person and I am living a very fulfilling and healthy life. For me, being gay has been an absolute blessing. Things that are most important to me are so because I am gay. I have John [his partner] and the house I live in, my friends. They would all be different if I were straight, but they wouldn't be any better.

All respondents consider their sexuality as God's creation. God created it and God sustains and blesses it. They have worked through the difficulty they initially faced and now believe that their sexuality, being God's creation, is as valid as heterosexuality. Clive is a financial professional in his mid-20s. Attending an Anglican church regularly, he argues:

> I think the fundamental question is whether God made us this way. Everything has to come down to it. There is no way that anyone else can claim that they were made by God heterosexual and then say that I was not made by God homosexual. There is simply no way that that can be said, because my experience of being homosexual is exactly the same as a straight person's experience as being heterosexual. It's

just the way we were made, there is nothing that has caused
this. It's just the way God has made us. It's not a sickness.
It's not unhealthy. It isn't inherently evil. There is no evil
flowing from it. It is just like being left-handed or red-haired.
It's unusual. It's different. It might be inconvenient like the
left-handed in the minority.

Clive's powerful argument is supported by many others, such as the
following:

I think, as I have said, God has made me who I am. I haven't been made the way I am, I believe, by my upbringing or
anything like that. It's the way I am. I honestly believe that
my orientation is in me. It's not something that's controlled
from somewhere else. (George, a Methodist in his late 30s)

A gay Christian is someone who happens to be a Christian,
whether they are gay, whether they are black or whether they
are yellow. I don't think it makes any difference because
what we are actually talking about is a state of being. I don't
think on the whole we are talking about a state of choice. I
don't think there is any choice in the matter. (Rick, an Anglican priest in his late 30s)

It is clear from these accounts that the respondents strongly believe
that their sexuality is not an outcome of nurture. Rather, it is a deliberate act of God who willed it that way. It is not a choice. It is a
divine given. Perceiving their sexuality from this perspective, the respondents consider the Church's stance on homosexuality ill-
founded.[4] To them, this unfavorable stance is predicated on the mis-
interpretation of the Scriptures that directly or indirectly allude to
homosexuality.[5] Thus, they actively challenge the Church's credibility
as their moral arbiter. The argument of Nigel, an engineering professional in his early 20s, typifies those of many:

I am amazed with the degree of ignorance there is in the
Church about what the Bible says about homosexuality. That
people who have been to university and who have studied
theology can come out with blatantly untrue things like Jesus
condemned homosexuality. You hear people saying this although they have been to theological college. This is utter
nonsense. I read the Old Testament. I read Leviticus and
Genesis. I find it quite incredible really that people can ex-
tract those texts and use them as excuses for saying that
therefore God hates homosexuals. I think it is intellectually
very unsound.

The de-contextualization of Biblical passages used by the Church appears to anger many respondents. To them, the Church uses these passages out of context to impose on them a moral code that is out-dated, without taking into consideration ever-changing social reality:

> I think to depend on something written several thousand years ago, written in a time, written by people who were to-tally different from us, I think it's foolish to be limited by it. To actually forego something that seems so perfectly right and natural because somebody at some time in a very specific context write against it, I think you'll do yourself great dam-age. I don't think one could argue that the Bible on its own favours homosexuality. What I do think though is that the homosexuality or the relationships that existed during Old Testament times and New Testament times were probably very different from the sort of relationships that exist now. Gay people probably didn't live in relationships during those times. There is no evidence they did or didn't. But one's guess is that they didn't. And Paul particularly is writing about gay prostitution in Corinthians, or wherever it is. But I think to argue that Scripture wasn't actually against homosexuality would be wrong. I think in fact it is. But it wasn't against the homosexuality that has developed, in loving relationships. It doesn't seem that it's loving relationships that is under at-tack in Scripture. A loving relationship is immensely positive and enriching as a Christian. (Simon, an administrator, late 40s)

> I just think that basically a lot of things in the Bible are to-tally out of date and have nothing to do with today. The Bible was written at the time, particularly the Old Testament, was written at the time for the needs of the Church at that time. There were laws to help the people cope with whatever the problems were at that particular time. And they were in a different country with a different civilization. So they were based on a code and were adapted to being what the hierar-chy decided, "This is what we wanted." The Bible, a lot of it is interpretation and as I said, a lot of it is down to what was needed at that time. The Bible and religion need to grow with the times. (George, civil servant, late 30s)

The Church, as a moral authority, is also greatly questioned by many respondents. Given that the Church has in the past directly or indirectly supported institutions which we now consider morally rep-rehensible, the respondents think that the Church is highly fallible in its teachings on homosexuality. James, an architect in his late 40s, argues strongly:

> I think basically on sexuality as a whole they are screwed up and they have got it wrong. The same with slavery, they have got it wrong. They have got it wrong as a human institution. The spirit is somehow for some reasons not revealed through the Church as a whole. They have got the issue wrong.

James is supported by Ron, a priest in the Church of England:

> I think the problem for being gay in the Church isn't that you have got a problem. It is the fact that the Church has got a problem. I think it's the same with women as well. The Church is having a problem with sex really, whether it's to do with women being ordained or with homosexual relationships. It's to do with sex which the Church just isn't very good at dealing with. I mean I have no problems at all with any of the biblical stuff. I mean I can go through blah blah blah and explain all the way. I have sort of read the books and written essays.

It is clear from these stories that the respondents have moved a long way from the guilt and shame they first felt. They have demonstrated the ability to not only overcome the pain, but also achieve victory in this battle, thus making the Church pale in its moral vocabulary.

### The Power of Personal Experience

The respondents' positive personal experiences as gay Christians and the fulfilling partnerships they have established play a pivotal role in the sustenance of their positive self-images. Drawing upon the strength of their personal experiences, many respondents justify the acceptability and validity of their sexuality:

> How can I possibly say what happens between Michael [his partner] and I is sinful? It's beyond me. It has been so liberating and enriching and sustaining. (Cliff, priest, partnership 2 years and 3 months old)

> Things [within the partnership] are getting better and better and better. That to me makes it clear that God has blessed the relationship. The things that I have been able to do in my vocation as a priest, the things that I have been able to give

of God to God's people springs out of what I have received from God through Michael [his partner]. (Robert, priest, partnership 16 years and 6 months old)

Having a faith, and I am living in an active faith, is so fundamental to who I am. I mean on an ethical basis apart from anything else. So we do behave in a very ethical manner towards each other. That makes our relationship much happier and we are always together. In a long term, we don't split up. We don't cheat on each other. We don't lie to each other. So it's an ethical faith. And then there are spiritual things. We have a common experience there. We have both shared the experience of being at the Eucharist, praying and being absolutely on tip-toe with excitement. Now we share that experience at the heart of our faith which is to do with belonging to the Christian community, belonging to the body of Christ, this fellowship. It binds us together more strongly because we are bonded together by this faith in Christ who is risen and in Christ who is present in the bread and the wine, and the gathered community around the altar. We share the excitement of them which is beyond the excitement of anything really. (Calvin, priest, partnership 5 years old)

Neil, a social worker who has been in a partnership for 14 years and 3 months also shares this confidence in his own positive experience:

Christianity is part of me. I endeavour to be a Christian and I try to incorporate Christian principles into my life. Therefore that has quite a lot of bearing on the things I do. I hope it affects the way I treat people to the better. Therefore it has got to influence the way I live with Damien [his partner], the way I treat Damien. Also in the early times, when we had problems in the relationship, I prayed for the relationship, and eventually things had been improved. And that's what made me convinced in myself. If it is against Christianity, if I prayed to God, I am not going to get help. But I have received help. I can't prove or show how I received help, but I have received help in this relationship when we needed it. If what we are doing is so totally against God, he wouldn't have answered my prayers.

James, an administrator, and Nigel, an engineering professional, have been together for 3 years and 3 months. They are one of the many couples who acknowledge the important role of Christianity in their partnership. Their Christian faith sustains them and makes the partnership work. Their positive experience informs them that it is possible to incorporate their Christianity and sexuality:

> *James*: I suppose the relationship actually arose, in many ways, out of the mutual belief and respect for spirituality. It has developed so much along those lines. It is difficult to imagine it anything other than that. Christianity does influence us because we have very strong feelings about it. We are often not in any sort of institutional setting and there is a lot of questioning. Our faith is very active and we both like that. That is a very important topic of conversation or feature of our relationship. And we still seek out time to free our spirits together, less overt than it used to be but we still do that. We met at the back of the church so I suppose we met in a spiritual and Christian context. Yes, that has always been a feature of our relationship and a very important one. [Spirituality] certainly was very important at the beginning and it was certainly something that we had very much in common. It is a very important part of our life together and it has meant that we pray together, we study together. We have worshipped outside together and worshipped alone together.

> *Nigel*: Well we wouldn't have started our relationship if it weren't for the fact that we were both striving after the truth. We are both Christian and we both wanted to know what it meant. In the early days we used to read the Bible together and pray together and went to church together. And now, we still pray together. But we don't pray in quite the same way, it's more in silence.... As Christians, we also try to be open to people, having our home as an open home that people can come into and stay. We also try to accept people as they are and also challenging ourselves and recognizing our own prejudices and tendency to judge. If James were a non-Christian, the relationship wouldn't have worked. It would have been difficult because we are both so passionate that it would be very difficult to have a partnership.

James and Nigel agree that the partnership began because of Christianity, and it is within this Christian framework that the partnership operates. Robert and Michael, both are priests, have been together for 16 years and 6 months. They uphold the same values.

> *Robert*: I think there is a problem in being a practicing gay Christian, certainly in that most of the churches are still saying you shouldn't be. I suppose God has called me to do two

things and that is both to be a Christian priest and to be in this relationship. I do think this is important. I have got a sense of vocation to Michael. One can be a gay person and one's relationship can be much of a way of holiness and as much a vocation as marriage for heterosexual Christians. And the relationship works. The fact that, in a way as everybody says this kind of relationship doesn't last, or you can't be a real Christian and do that kind of thing, the fact that it does last and does work is in a sense an important proof. That's what makes you feel confident.

*Michael*: The Church and its latest official statement about homosexuality is that as being, if you are a Roman Catholic, an intrinsic disorder. I cannot accept that from the experience of being me and what has been achieved in my life as a result of me being me. I am just being me. God is part of my life and I don't consider that to be an intrinsic disorder. I believe it is possible to be homosexual and Christian and living in a relationship.

The above accounts sufficiently demonstrate the emphasis these respondents place on personal experiences as the basis of their moral choices. John Hannigan calls this emphasis on personal religious experiences the "theology of experience," in place of the "theology of authority" that emphasizes religious dogma.[6] This "theology of experience" can be seen in operation in Simon's argument:

As I have grown more confident in the past ten years into, I think, matured in the Christian religion, I actually rely on my own experience. If my own experience and everything I know and understand show me St. Paul on this issue and others were mistaken, well there it is. I am arrogant enough to put my own understanding, my own experience, up against any sort of written Thou Shalt Not or whatever.

## MANAGING THE RELATIONSHIP WITH LOCAL CHURCHES

Having rejected the Church's teachings on homosexuality, and therefore the perceived incompatibility between their sexual and religious identities, how do these gay Christians relate to the local churches? Do they regularly attend local churches? Do they stay away altogether? Or do they carefully select certain churches? These are some of the questions that I will answer in this section.

## Why Leave the Church?

Some respondents have distanced themselves from the local churches, precipitated by their disappointment with the lack of progress in the Church's treating of the issue of homosexuality. None of the respondents I interviewed say that their distancing is an outcome of fear of exposing their sexuality or partnership. All, having been to the church, have now distanced themselves from it as an act of rejection of the Church as an institution and its moral authority.

James and Nigel, who met in a local church and used to attend the same church, decided to distance themselves two years before I interviewed them. James still considers himself a member of the Church of England, while Nigel now considers himself a "nondenominational Christian":

*James*: I come from a very evangelical Anglican tradition. I want to be in the Church. But what I feel angry about is the intolerance and the promotion of views by people who have no understanding and have not sought to gain much understanding and experience of gay people before making pronouncements and creating organisations that set out to undermine gay people. To be honest with you, I would much rather be hated than to have this kind of "loving" Christianity thrust upon me, which is the feature of some of the Church. I find that appalling and totally unacceptable. I therefore feel that my place at the moment is outside the Church, much more into an individual making my way to God. So I stopped being active in the established Church. I am questioning the traditional approach. Do we need the traditional base of churches? Do we need the institution of the Church? Do we need a vast amount of tradition which actually seems to handicap us?

*Nigel*: I think for too long we both went to the church due to a sense of guilt, that we ought to go to church. I feel very healthy to be taking time out from going to the church now. We stopped about two years ago. I can't bring myself to saying the liturgy because the God that is portrayed has nothing to do with the God that I believe. The self-hatred in the Anglican liturgy, the obsession with penitence I find very difficult. I think I started to think about it quite a long time ago. But I continued to go. I would just sit through the whole session and think, I don't think there is anything for me. Besides my sexuality, I also had to deal with my attitudes to the Scriptures and the Church as an institution and my image of God. I realized that my image of who God is doesn't tie in with the image of God presented in the Church that I have been to.

Their disillusion with the Church precipitates the need to practice Christianity in an individualized manner. To keep their Christian faith, they have to, ironically, distance themselves from the Church, the supposed institution for religious instructions and guidance. They tell me that they have never had any negative experiences with the local church because of their sexuality and partnership. Another respondent who is highly critical of the Church's credibility asserts:

> This is one of the reasons why I don't go to church. That's one of the reasons I don't believe in the Church. It is teaching all these negative things about homosexuality and basically putting down gays. There is so much hypocrisy within the Church when there is like 30 percent of the clergy in the Church [of England] are gay, yet in the General Synod they vote in all these anti-gay things. And these people are telling you to trust in them! So I am pretty anti-Church. In the Church there are nice people individually, but the institution I am anti. (Francis, mid-30s, a member of the Church of England)

Charles, a manager in his mid-20s, also argues about his need to distance himself from the Roman Catholic Church:

> I believe in the basics of Christian teachings. But I don't practice the Catholic faith although I do believe in it, mainly because if I do, I am in a way persecuting gays because of what they [the Roman Catholic Church] did in the past, and because of their attitude towards not just gays but also towards a lot of other issues. I feel if I go to a Catholic church, then I am colluding with what they are saying and doing. At the moment I distance myself from it. I left the Church because of that. My Catholic faith is very separated from the Church. I don't feel at home in the Church.

Nigel, a former Church of England priest who left the pastoral ministry after six years, bitterly expresses the same sentiment. He considers himself a victim of stigmatization:

> I had a difficulty with my senior colleague. He chose to reveal the nature of my relationship with Alan [his partner] to my Bishop. I felt that was such a gross betrayal. And then the Bishop was hopeless in dealing with it. So I didn't want to belong to an institution that is capable of that sort of be-

trayal. So I resigned. It was an awful time. I am still bitterly
upset about it.

It is clear that the respondents' distancing themselves from the
local church is not an outcome of fear of exposure. Rather, it is a deliberate rejection of the Church as an institution, precipitated by a
positive self-image which makes the Church's argument against homosexuality increasingly unjustifiable.


## Fully Accepted

In spite of the fact that this is a rare minority, some respondents
are in the fortunate position that their sexuality and partnership do
not bring any stigmatization in the local church. The positive and
accepting church climate is the most significant reason why they actively participate in church activity and make no secret of their sexuality and partnership.

The Quakers have long had a liberal tradition, accepting of peo-
ples from diverse backgrounds. Two respondents who attend Quaker
meetings testify about the link between the accepting climate and
their willingness to completely disclose information about themselves. Kirk, a retiree above 70 years old, recounts his experience:

> In my former church, the isolation became so great and so
> many of us were rejected. Everybody was an outcast as ho-
> mosexuals in those days, in the 1930s. I saw that there could
> be no future for me. I was very unhappy. [After a five-year
> lapse] I started going to Quaker meetings. I just sat there
> quietly and became relaxed, and all my irritations of life, they
> all subsided. It offers a very good atmosphere. I find support
> there. We don't have the usual form of worship. We have no
> hymns. We have no pastor. We just go and sit inside. You
> open up yourself. You relax and be quiet and wait for the
> Holy Spirit to move in you. Some people are moved to speak
> or pray.

Kirk's partner, Simon, a retiree also above 70 years old, does not go
to any church at present. He was, however, actively involved in a
Methodist church. Nigel, a lecturer in his 50s, also goes to Quaker
meetings. His partner, Paul, attends an Anglican church due to personal preference. Nigel explains:

> Quakers are not formally tied to things like the Nicene Creed.
> Also with the theological change and re-thinking in me, I find
> the Society of Friends more appropriate. It offers me a free

environment to express my faith. In my former church, you couldn't talk freely about your sexuality in the open.

Simon, an administrator in his late 30s, left the church for 15 years because "it is an anachronism." But now he is actively involved in a Church of England parish church for about four hours a week. He is the church warden, scriptural reader, and occasional lay preacher. The gay-friendly climate of his church is certainly the main reason for his high degree of involvement. He states:

I just happened to go into [church's name] and [priest's name] happened to say hello to me. I thought he was a nice man. And I came back for the Sunday Service. I ran into him again and stayed. It was purely on the strength of his personality. [Church's name] is known to be very very open to gay people, and [priest's name] is a gay priest and the church warden is also gay. And although that's more hidden I think, there is still this sort of welcome. Also, it gives me a lot of scope to do things within the church. So it's supportive on the gay level and all sorts of other levels as well.

There could be a discrepancy between what the Church authority officially pronounces about homosexuality and the climate of a local church. In spite of the negative stance adopted by the Roman Catholic Church authority, the local Catholic church which Alan and Jon have been attending for 14 years is extremely friendly and accepting. The acceptance and affirmation they find in the church encourage them to be exceptionally active in the administration of the church.

*Alan* [he spends at least six hours per week on church work]: Just about the first week we turned up, we were made welcome. Nobody has ever made the faintest hint of protest about us being gay. We went there by chance for a baptism, and we immediately felt that we liked it and it was a nice atmosphere. So a few weeks later we went back for the service. We felt so much more comfortable and more at home and more welcome there. We both help the vicar with various things because she's a good friend of ours so it's easy to help her do things. So we are very involved indeed. I'm also the unofficial doctor of most of the congregation. So it's a close relationship with the church and with the congregation.

*Jon* [he just completed a 3-year term as church warden, still sits on the church council]: We were encouraged by the support we get from the church to our relationship. When we were at [former church], we were not encouraged at all. We are definitely more at home at [present church]. The church every year makes a small contribution to the LGCM [Lesbian and Gay Christian Movement] and to one or two AIDS charities because it feels that it's important to build solidarity with a disadvantaged group within the church.

However, the discrepancy between the negative official position of the Church and the accepting climate of the local church can also backfire. This is the experience of Luke and Mark, who have been attending a Methodist church for six years. They decided to leave their positive church because of the negative official stance taken by the Methodist Conference. Luke explains:

We have decided to resign from our membership because it's discriminatory against me as a gay person. We have immense difficulty. The church we go to is an open, honest, liberal church. We have been accepted fully for what we are. I don't feel vulnerable at all at the local church. The hierarchy, the Conference, is different. It is also safe to say that within the circuit to which our church belongs there are certain ministers and officers who are very homophobic. We struggled about what we would do. I can't stay in the Methodist Church, knowing that it disapproves of my relationship despite the full approval of my local church, because someone in the local church can say, "The Conference decision has effect here and we think you should toe the line." I am very sure I can't stay in this kind of setup where we live in the mercy of the Conference, or waiting for the next minister to come who may be homophobic. There is a great sense of insecurity.

My post-interview contact with Luke and Mark confirms that they have resigned from their church membership. They now attend the Metropolitan Community Church, which is widely known for its open policy to the gay community. In this particular case, the complete integration into the local church is terminated by the discrepancy between the climate of the official stance and that of the local church. It is exactly this kind of discrepancy that disappoints the respondents and discredits the respectability of the Church in their eyes.

## Keeping Quiet

If a positive local church provides the respondents with confidence to disclose information about themselves, a negative local church climate effects the completely opposite result. Some respondents choose to keep completely quiet about themselves. Having no one who is cognizant of their situation, they experience no sense of support. In the worst possible scenario, a couple who attend the same church might need to orchestrate the presentation of their relationship as "just two good friends." Needless to say, this imposes on them great psychological strains. There is always the need to manipulate their image as a pair of good friends and yet not too close as to project an image of a couple.

A good example in this case is Richard and George, who attend the same Methodist church. They perceive the church to be quite negative. This enforces the need to opt for complete concealment of their partnership in the church. Their situation is exacerbated by the fact that Richard is married. Both have so far never encountered any negative experiences, and they do not feel vulnerable. They are certain that although there might be church members who suspect, the majority of the congregation remains in the dark insofar as their partnership is concerned:

*Richard*: No. One or two people have made comments about the fact that George and I have gone on holidays without my wife. There are one or two women that used to work with me at Sunday school who would say, "What a strange relationship." But I wouldn't challenge them or ask what they meant and they wouldn't make any further comment.

*George*: Well they know that we are friendly. Whenever they see one, there is always the other one. They don't know that we are a gay partnership. I mean some of them might guess. They all know Richard is married. They all know that I am around. Whether they guess any more than that I don't know.

Richard and George are sanguine about their ability in handling the possible enquiry into their discreetly presented "friendship." This confidence appears to rest on their belief in the mutual respect for privacy. In response to the question of what they would do if their "friendship" is under question, they explain:

*Richard*: As I said to you there was one person who obviously doubted [about their relationship] but most people, really in a sense it is up to them. I would acknowledge that relationship as much as it needs to be acknowledged in front of people. I don't ask them about their sex life or whatever. So I assume that my sex life is not of interest to them. It might well be, but that is their problem, not mine. They should ac-

knowledge our friendship, our closeness to one another. What
they want to take out of that is up to them.

*George*: I don't know. I think it depends on who it was. I
mean there are a lot of people that we talk to about everything, more closely than others. I really don't know. If they
are asking, I would assume they are asking out of friendli-
ness, not out of aggression. If it is out of aggression, I would
ask them to mind their own business.

Neil attends a Catholic church while his partner, Damien, has
left the church for 13 years due to his disappointment with the
church on the whole. Neil perceives his church to be homophobic, although he has never had any negative experiences. Opting for complete concealment is therefore a necessity to him:

In my local church, the priest is an old-fashioned sort of priest
and he wouldn't entertain it [homosexuality] at all. The congregation don't know either. I haven't encountered any hostil-
ity. What I have encountered is I think hard to describe. People who have gone through it will understand it, sort of a cold
shoulder. Nobody wants to know you. I feel vulnerable. They
aren't friendly anyway, but they are a little bit more friendly
to other people. I have been going on and off to this church
since 1987. But I don't know anyone round there, not even to
speak to. <And yet you continue going?> I go basically because it is convenient. It is just round the corner. I am not going there for the people. I am going there because I need to
pray and I need to worship God. I do feel that the environment can be quite homophobic. I think I am highly identifi-
able for what I am. I think I probably look gay. Probably
people put two and two together. They have decided what I
am and that is what makes the barrier.

It is interesting to note the two different reasons for complete
concealment between Richard and George, and Neil. They have never
had any negative experiences in their respective churches. However,
Richard and George do not feel vulnerable or threatened and are confident about their ability to face up to any potential challenge. On the
other hand, Neil uses the same strategy out of a sense of vulnerability. What distinguishes their motivations is the presence or absence
of a sense of vulnerability and the confidence of being in control of the
situation.

## Telling Those Who Need to Know

This seems to be the most common situation in which most respondents find themselves. Singling out a selective few is a means of protecting the dissemination of the information to the entire church and, on the other hand, securing the support of that small circle of individuals. This helps prevent their sense of total alienation from the church as far as their partnership is concerned. This will also make the presentation of the relationship before the church less demanding.

The selected audience to whom such information is disclosed are, expectedly, close and supportive friends in the congregation. In some cases, the priest also becomes the object of disclosure, having been observed by the respondents as being accepting and supportive. Cliff, a Church of England priest in his mid-40s, shares his experience:

> It seems to me the church reacts positively. How far they know exactly what our relationship is, of course, something else. But then we are quite careful not to offend. We are just relaxed with how we are with them. I mean I think what they observe is, Michael [his partner] was someone who looked after me when I was ill. They see him as a sort of good friend and supporter, someone who helped me along the line. I doubt that I have exercised their minds to anything beyond that. They might feel that we are actually a little bit more special than that. They don't seem to mind. Certainly we have no hassle from people. They have been very kind and generous. I don't feel threatened. It is useful to have Michael as part of the community anyway. He is there and they see him in his own right. He is being himself doing his own things. I think that is very positive. I hope they see it as a very positive part of my life. Anything else is between Michael and I really.

In the case of Moses and Ron, Moses attends the church in which Ron is one of the priests. Some of Ron's colleagues know about the nature of their relationship and are quite supportive. He therefore is not too concerned about being stigmatized at his workplace. However, this means that Moses has to keep a low profile in the church in order not to raise suspicion. This is not as easy as it sounds, as they tell their story:

> *Ron*: It [being a gay priest] is a very bizarre existence. It's not a very good existence in terms of the pressures it puts on you. I mean you can't, as a gay person, lead that sort of lifestyle that you might want to. You can't live where you want to live.

This is not where I'd choose to live [the church-provided accommodation is very near the church]. I mean the house goes with the job. I mean those are the sorts of complications I am in.

*Moses*: You see, I listen to a lot of gay clergy saying how difficult it is to be gay and a priest. But I lose patience with the argument. I think it is probably more difficult for me because if I answer the front door [they live together], it is very difficult for me to say who I am. But he [Ron] can say he is the vicar. And if I went to church and somebody said, "Hello where do you live?" It's difficult for me. It's difficult for me to be on the electoral roll in the church, because that would mean that my name will be on the official document which would say who I am or where I live.

Moses' account highlights the peculiar difficulty experienced by couples in which one or both of the partners are clergy. In the latter case, cohabitation is not possible unless one of the partners gives up the pastoral profession. In both cases, the support of a few understanding individuals in the church is therefore of paramount importance.

Two factors encourage the respondents to gradually disclose information about themselves: the availability of support from a few individuals, and their own confidence. The availability of some degree of support is reciprocated by a high degree of discretion. Calvin is a Church of England priest, new to his parish. Clive, his partner, has recently moved into the accommodation provided by the church and attends the church where Calvin works. Clive is introduced to the church as Calvin's "lodger" and "good friend." They tell their story:

*Calvin*: The vicar does know [about their partnership] but the members of the congregation don't. The intention is that they will never be told publicly because some of them will feel very shocked. But at the same time we hope that Clive will become a member of this church. He can be seen as my lodger because you can get away with that in this part of [city]. That's all right. Maybe five years from now the vicar will go round and say, "Did you know Calvin and Clive were gay?" They might say, "I suppose we did really." My vicar is great so he is supporting me. But we are not going to confront people. There may be people whom I will get to know enough to tell along the way. If somebody asked about us, it probably depends on who it was and in what ways they asked. I certainly wouldn't tell him straight off. I don't think I would be as blunt as to say, "This is none of your business," because as a priest in a way it is their business because I belong to the Christian community. But I suspect I would beat around the bush a bit and try to leave things ambiguous. Now whether that is possible depends on who asks me and how well I know that person and how I think he is going to respond and why he is asking.

*Clive*: Yes, the vicar is accepting. He has been very nice, very welcoming. He seems to be a nice person. So I think what needs to happen now and in the future is just to have a little bit of time, take things slowly, keep a low profile. But it is very difficult to make genuine friends without them. I have no idea how it will work out.

It is obvious from the accounts above that having the confidence in the church climate in general does encourage information disclosure, as in the case of Rick, a Church of England priest. His partner, Walter, attends the church he pastors. Rick explains the importance of support:

It [being questioned by parishioners] wouldn't worry me. I think the fact that my boss [the bishop] knows helps. I think he quite likes Walter, sort of fairly supportive, although he never asks us any questions and doesn't make life difficult for us. He knows that Walter lives here. He knows that we are lovers. Sometimes he asks how Walter is. He was quite concerned when Walter lost his job and things like that. No. We don't feel threatened. [In the church] I don't tell everybody. It depends on how close I am to them. I weigh up their attitudes on other subjects. If they tend to be liberal and easygoing, I'm more inclined to tell them.

Having the confidence in some supportive individuals obviously helps the respondents in organizing their relationship with the church. However, personal confidence in their own ability to face up to potential challenge also encourages disclosure. Paul, who attends a Catholic church, has a strong personality and is prepared to face potential challenges from the church with a fierce response:

I don't care. I feel I am all right. If someone challenges me, I will retaliate. I would say, "Yes I am. So what? What the fuck has it got to do with you?" That will terrify them because the people who do that are trying to push you around. They always think that people like me are weak. So when you turn your aggression back, they are absolutely terrified.

Similarly, Samuel, who attends a Catholic church, also expresses this air of confidence:

> Nobody has ever come up to me and asked me about it or even hinted at it. I never have any problems. I don't feel vulnerable. I may feel embarrassed I think. If somebody in the parish came up and said, "Look, are you two gays?" I would feel slightly embarrassed. But that is just my age. I am in that generation that grew up before the law reform and everything. I would feel slightly embarrassed but I think I will cope with it all right. I would probably say, "Well yes, but why are you so bothered about it? It's not bothering me."

The stories I have told in this chapter clearly demonstrate that these gay Christians have indeed transcended above their circumstances. In spite of the unfavorable stance of the Church on homosexuality, they have developed a positive self-image and incorporated their spirituality and sexuality harmoniously. This positive outlook, buttressed by personal experiences, generates a tremendous justificatory power for the acceptability of their sexuality and partnership.

## CHAPTER 7

# Networking: Participation in the Gay Subculture

In the previous chapter, I discussed the difficulty that gay Christians, as individuals and couples, encounter in relating to the local churches. Managing their identity in a potentially stigmatizing social environment is a demanding task. In this chapter, the discussion focuses on the gay subculture, a different kind of social environment. A social environment that, by definition, should provide the participants with support and the opportunity for networking.

## GAY CHRISTIAN GROUPS

Slightly more than one-half of the 60 individual respondents I interviewed are affiliated to at least one gay Christian group. However, almost one-half of them are passive members who do not participate in any form of activity. They merely make financial contributions and in return receive information about the groups concerned. The others participate in these groups with a varying degree of activeness.

### Why Participate?

Most of the respondents participate in these groups because, through them, they can provide and receive much-needed moral and emotional support. These groups are therefore viewed as "expressive groups," which offer them a common platform for social contact without having to conceal their sexuality.[1] This generates a sense of community and also helps them dispel a potential sense of alienation in the church or their daily life.

James and Nigel are both actively involved in the Lesbian and Gay Christians Movement (LGCM). Nigel, an engineering professional in his early 20s, is also involved in the work of the Institute for the Study of Christianity and Sexuality (ISCS, now Centre for the Study of Christianity and Sexuality, CSCS). He says:

> I think they [gay Christian groups] are a lifeline to many people because the major problem for some gays but specifically for gay Christians is one of isolation, the fear that they are the only people in the world to be inflicted with this terrible "sin." I think it's so important that LGCM exists so that people know that there are others out there. That's the most important thing.

*There are others out there* encapsulates the sentiment succinctly. The existence of these groups gives gay Christians a sense of community that supports their often lonely and isolating existence. Alan, a medical professional in his late 40s, who is involved with the LGCM with his partner, also expresses this point:

> I think they are very important. It's nice to know that they exist for us. But for a lot of people, they feel very lonely. I think it is vital to know that they exist and that they can go and join in. If you go to a meeting like the LGCM, you meet all sorts of people who are obviously very lonely people. The LGCM might be the only support and Christian display of love they get.

Alan's view is supported by Neil, who was actively involved in QUEST (an organization for Catholic gays and lesbians) but is now a passive member. He does not feel the need for support now because of his partnership with Damien. However, he acknowledges the importance of such support.

> It's a meeting point for people who would be isolated and I can tell you that because in 1976 when I first came into contact with QUEST, it basically let me know that there are other people around, you know, when you don't feel there is anybody else. It's moral support. You know eventually you can make a date to go and meet somebody, to have a chat with somebody.

The need for moral support is probably more acute for gay priests, whose profession exerts great pressure on them to conceal social information about themselves, although this is contingent upon the climate of the local church itself, as I have discussed in Chapter 6. This is especially important for gay priests serving in provincial areas. Aaron, in his mid-30s, is a member of the Anglican Clergy Consultation (ACC), which is a support group for Church of England priests and their partners. He asserts:

> I mean the ACC also supports clergy who find themselves out on a limb. It's all right for those of us who are in London or in other cities with a gay population. But imagine you are stuck in the wilds in the countryside, living miles from the kindred spirit. It must be good to know that you are together with a group where there are other gay clergy.

The participation in gay Christian groups is clearly a means of establishing a support network. Calvin, a priest, and Clive, a financial professional, are both members of the LGCM. They acknowledge the importance of this networking:

> *Calvin*: It reminds you that there are people out there living the same way. It is a support network. It lets you know all the news. It lets you know that people who are gays like you are being arrested or tortured. I feel that I belong to them and I owe them something because they are like my blood brothers and sisters. That is like a family I belong to.

> *Clive*: It is a network, isn't it? LGCM opens a new gateway of meeting people of different generations. You know, through LGCM, I have met couples who have been together for 40 years. It is an encouragement to me.

Charles, an administrator in his mid-20s, participates in the LGCM monthly local meetings. He is also a volunteer for the LGCM telephone helpline. Besides receiving support, he also sees it as an opportunity to offer assistance to other gay Christians. A sense of community is apparent in his account:

> Working on the helpline had made me aware of the problems of gay Christians. I wasn't really aware of a lot of them, especially for clergy. You get a lot of clergy ringing up about personal problems. I get a lot of satisfaction out of talking and helping other people coming to terms with being gay and Christian. On the whole I just listen and I find that very helpful for me.

Gay Christian groups also offer a safe environment for the participants to practice both their sexuality and Christianity. This consolidates and affirms the compatibility of being gay and Christian. Richard and George, for instance, are drawn to the LGCM and a local lesbian and gay Christian group for this reason.

> *Richard*: It [LGCM] is almost like a fellowship group. You can go there and you can acknowledge that you are Christian and you can acknowledge you are gay. Those two things don't always hang very easily together. In any organizations, to say that you are gay and Christian makes you a bit of an outsider. Therefore it is good to be able to come to something that you can actually be totally honest. It is obviously very important. Being a Christian and being gay are obviously two of the most important parts of our lives, and therefore to be able to go to a group which actually accepts you as a Christian and accepts you as a gay at the same time is brilliant. You know, not to be apologizing for what you are, but to say, you know, I can be a Christian and gay.

> *George*: Certainly I find the LGCM helpful. I find it a comfort to know that there are Christians around and they are respected in their own rights for their beliefs or whatever.

Rick, a priest in his late 30s, is an active member of LGCM. He also acknowledges the importance of a safe environment for both sexuality and spirituality:

> Well I think they provide the only welcoming group of people that can actually help Christians assimilate their faith and their sexuality rather than either reject their sexuality or reject their faith. So they do provide for gay Christians who want to grow and mature. They are a sort of reference group to do it.

Some respondents also use their participation in gay Christian groups to effect positive change by engaging in dialogue with the church specifically. Rick, whose view I have just presented above, also holds an important official position in an umbrella organization for lesbian and gay groups in a locality. He strongly believes in the ability of these groups to effect change through campaigning within the Christian community. He argues:

> With [the abovementioned organization], I am the [official position] and I have been on the working party which is looking at ways in which gay people in the dioceses of [city] can have

their views represented. In particular, we are looking at the Bishop of [city]'s [official document] where he puts forward the plan for the dioceses. What we are doing is that we are questioning the whole absence of anything to do with social justice or treatment of minorities or looking at the problem of homosexuality. [The organization] wants the Diocese of [city] to concentrate on the problem of homophobia, because we don't believe that essentially there is a problem of homosexuality, but there is a problem with intolerance. I think the Church is deep in prejudice and ignorance.

In agreement, Warren, an editor who is involved with the LGCM, also emphasizes this socio-political role of gay Christian groups:

I think it's good for its members. They are also a campaigning group, because just left to its devices, there will be enough people in the Church who would like to keep quiet, not to be bothered to think about anything. So very undoubtedly LGCM does dig some people up their wrong way. But nevertheless keeps the issue going.

An interesting observation is that some respondents refuse to be affiliated to *certain* gay Christian groups because of their disagreement with their operational objective and theological foundation. This reflects the ideological diversity among gay Christians.

The LGCM, for instance, is rejected by some on the ground that it is becoming too preoccupied with its political agenda, and it lacks a sound theological base. Morgan, a retired lecturer in his 70s, stopped his affiliation to LGCM ten years ago. He argues:

Because it has broadened increasingly into the political sphere which I don't agree with. It is confrontational. It was a movement which seems to be to get roughly balanced between a campaign and a church movement. The very fact that I don't go to those things anymore much suggests that I think the balance has gone wrong.

On theological ground, the LGCM has also received some opposition, which leads to some respondents' disassociation from it. This is characterized by the argument of Robert, a priest, who prefers QUEST to the LGCM:

I won't join the LGCM because I don't believe it develops a theology for gay relationships. I believe very strongly that one has to have a strong sacramental theology for sex if one is really going to say this is a Christian gay movement. LGCM has always stopped short of that. They have never been prepared to put across a monogamous ethic. They have not been willing to say that for Christians you really should stick with one partner. I think faithfulness to one person actually is quite a profound thing. I don't think it is just a social convention. It's something that affects who we are and the people we grow into. It has something to do with the fact that we are made in God's image and that we are capable of faithfulness. The LGCM doesn't put this forward. I am more tied in for QUEST because it has a clear theological structure. My impression is that they take much more seriously the tradition of the Church and they work much harder at engaging with that. I think they have come to the view that it has got to be basically a monogamous structure if you ever want to fit a gay relationship into the tradition or into the teaching. I think QUEST has got it right.

While some respondents accept certain gay Christian groups and reject others, certain respondents think that all these groups should work with a common goal to improve the plight of all gay Christians, despite their diverse strategies and emphases. Ricky and Samuel are both members of QUEST, and Ricky is also affiliated to the LGCM. They acknowledge the importance of diversity.

*Ricky*: QUEST is more diplomatic. It has a different way of approaching problems. LGCM tends to be more confrontational whereas QUEST will challenge and enter into dialogue. But we need all. I don't think QUEST is too soft. It just has got a different style and a more polite way of dealing with problems. But I would never disparage the avant garde. We need them. They are all important.

*Samuel*: I think they have a lot to contribute. They are valuable and important institutions to help people to come to terms with the conflict they often feel between their sexuality and their religion. QUEST is very good for the kind of people who come to QUEST. And LGCM is very very good for a rather different kind of people, probably a little bit more socialist, left-wing, militant.

## Why Stay Away?

Most of the respondents I interviewed are not affiliated to gay Christian groups. While lack of time appears to be the general reason for this, some respondents also specifically mention that their nonparticipation is precipitated by the fact that their need for support and companionship is fulfilled within the partnership and/or the wider circle of gay or heterosexual friends, in or outside the church. Thus, participation in these groups is not a priority, as some argue:

> I don't have to socialize, I mean I have got this partnership with Tom [his partner] for one thing, and mostly they are single guys because of [the need of] company I think. I don't need that. (James, architect, late 40s, partnership 16 years old)

> I belong to a substantial number of church groups. I do have so many gay clergy friends whom I meet as a matter of calls. So I don't feel I have to join a group. Well I have joined the gay group called the Church of England. Certainly a lot of gay clergy. Yes! (Aaron, priest, mid-30s, partnership 13 years old)

These accounts speak for the strength the respondents have derived from their partnerships and the support of people around. Some respondents stay away from gay Christian groups because of their concern about the ghettoization of gay people: the formation of a separatist community. Their assimilationist approach interests them in a wider community where people of all sexualities can relate to one another harmoniously.[2] David, a Roman Catholic priest, and his partner Simon, a teacher, distance themselves from all gay groups, religious and nonreligious. David asserts:

> I don't feel attracted towards things specifically for gay people. My ideal is to be able to be gay in a totally open sort of community where people can be what they want to be, instead of living in a ghetto. It seems so artificial to me, that's the trouble. In the sense that when a lot of gay people get together, that seems to be a limited sort of experience. I just like to be with people where one can be gay but other people are not gay.

This concern about ghettoization is shared by another couple, Cliff and Michael. Michael, a medical professional, is uninterested in these groups principally because of his heavy work commitment. Cliff, on the other hand, was once an active member of LGCM until two years ago, when he officially terminated his affiliation. He explains:

> I got really fed-up with it. I think I have quite a strong objection to thinking that being gay is the most important thing for myself and therefore it should be in any sense sort of limits and defines me. I think it is helpful to me to be able to say, "Yes I am gay," because this is to recognize the sexual

aspect about myself. But I can't stand people who sort of must have gay electrician, gay hair-dresser. This is nonsense.

David's concern for not wanting to be defined and limited solely by his sexuality is shared by Neil and Damien. Neil, a social worker, argues that his needs of companionship and support are fulfilled in the partnership; thus there is no need to participate in these groups. Damien, also a social worker, argues his concern about ghettoization vociferously:

> What worries me is that gay people are falling into the trap of labeling themselves with a name like that. Labeling themselves with a word like "gay" to counteract people calling us "queer" or "homosexual" or whatever. But they are falling into a trap too. Why should you describe your whole personality, the whole reality of your existence in this life, by your sexual orientation only? Even gay people, because they are fighting for their rights, are being classified as "poofters" or "queers" or whatever. They are written off simply because of their sexual orientation. People utter those words in utter disgust and resentment and hatred, you see. And then gay people are trying to defend themselves because of their sexual orientation, and they have forgotten the rest of what they are, their personality, their gifts, their intelligence, the work that they do.

Finally, a few respondents refuse to participate in gay Christian groups for fear of exposure. Although these groups offer a comparatively safe environment, there is the concern that information of their presence might be used against them. This concern is clearly expressed below:

> I think the problem is, most of the time we never told anybody about us. It's fairly recently that we don't have a problem talking about us with other people. The thought of going to a gay group of about 100 gay clergy [referring to the ACC] would be horrific really. I suppose the thing is, we want to actually choose to reveal what we want about ourselves, to whom we want, rather than belonging to an organization which you have to reveal things just by belonging to it. We want to be in control. (Ron, a priest, mid-30s)

The above response highlights the couple's use of nonparticipation as a way to control the information about themselves. By belonging to a group, one loses that control to a certain extent. That proves to be a cause for concern and a justification for nonparticipation. This reason, however, is cited by very few respondents.

## NON-CHRISTIAN GAY GROUPS

Even fewer respondents participate in non-Christian gay groups. Only 7 of the 60 respondents I interviewed participate in these groups on a regular basis. The remainder consists of a majority of those who are completely withdrawn from these groups and a minority who merely support them financially. On the couple level, none are jointly affiliated to any groups.

The respondents are highly inclined to perceive non-Christian groups in terms of the socio-political role. While they regard gay Christian groups as a safe environment for moral and emotional support, non-Christians gay groups are viewed primarily as the agents for effecting social change.

Jackson, a financial professional in his late 20s, is highly committed to equal opportunities in all contexts. Equality to him is an important Christian principle to uphold. An active member of STONEWALL (a legal reform lobbying group), he argues:

> I think it is important. I mean yes in a way it relates directly to my faith because it is a gospel issue at stake about the dignity of human beings. Human beings are demanding their dignity from their oppressors, against their oppressors. It is a tragedy that the Church has alienated these people for so many years. So okay we just have to forget religion and fight for the rights that God would have given them if someone else hasn't stripped them of them.

In spite of the non-religious nature of STONEWALL, it is clear from Jackson's account that it does address a similar issue in this case: a minority oppressed by the society (including the Church) on the ground of their sexuality. In this case, the oppression needs to be dispelled, regardless of the religious beliefs. His support for STONEWALL is echoed by Samuel, who is also a member of STONEWALL and TORCHE (Tory Campaign for Gay Equality), another lobbying group.

> STONEWALL has potentially been politically quite effective. They have been able to speak in a way that politicians and even the Prime Minister actually listen. So that's important. Again I think it is important to individuals. But what is most important is raising public awareness of the reality of gay people in society. There is always a need in society for minority groups to make more noise in order not to be totally marginalized. People need to be aware that there are a large number of gay people in society. If you don't have somebody

making a noise about it, then all the prejudices just go on un-
challenged.

Both respondents acknowledge the potential of STONEWALL for
legal reform through their lobbying activities; thus their participation.
They do not seek to incorporate into the mainstream society by
merely living passively with the stigma of being gay, but to actively
redefine themselves and educate society to accept this self-definition.

Some respondents regard participation in these groups as an opportunity to meet potential sex partners. Groups such as the London
Gay Swimming Club, the Gay Dining Club and the Gay Nudity Club,
established for social rather than political purposes, are used by
some respondents as a means for potential recreational sex, a possible starting point for a relationship. Kirk, in his 70s, is an active
member of such social groups. He stopped participating in a gay
Christian group because his need in this area was not met. He now
regularly participates in these social groups:

> The primary objective in participating in their activities is to
> make contacts, and not so much for support from the gay
> community. What I just need is gay fulfilment of one sort or
> another. Usually that starts with an actual sexual experi-
> ence. It may continue into a wider friendship or it may not.

**Gay Pride March**

Some respondents also see the benefits of participating in the
annual Gay Pride March. Alan, a medical professional in his late
40s, participates in the march almost every year. He says:

> Going to the Gay Pride whenever I am in London is the only
> public gay thing I do. I like to go. I have a lovely time. It's
> great fun walking down the road being a real nuisance and
> holding up all the traffic. For one day in a year, all of central
> London has to recognize that there are thousands of gays. It's
> lovely. If it did it every Saturday I think it would be a nui-
> sance and stupid, but one day in a year is nice to show them
> that there are lots of us and we are having fun.

Alan's view is supported by the following typical accounts:

> The Gay Pride March is the one occasion in a year that we all
> get together. Nice perfect day out. People can enjoy them-
> selves. It is all free. It's actually quite uplifting to be able to
> walk along the streets of London surrounded by other gay

people, just saying we are here. I think it is quite amazing. (Francis, computing professional, mid-30s)

I think the Gay Pride can be split into two distinct parts, which is the march as the political message and the party afterwards, which is the social side. I think that's a very good combination because it combines two different events. But it conveys two positive messages which I think is important for both of these views to get across. (Paul, civil servant, late 20s)

These accounts clearly demonstrate the importance of the march in two aspects. First, it is a political event organized to demonstrate to the public the existence of gay people as an oppressed minority. Second, it is also a social event in which gay people and their supportive heterosexual friends are able to foster a sense of community, thus reinforcing their identity.[3]

## COMMERCIAL GAY SCENE

In this case, I refer the commercial gay scene to four types of establishments: gay bars/pubs, gay baths/saunas, gay discos, and gay bookstores. On the whole, 119 of the respondents (87.5 percent) report that they have been to the commercial gay scene before at least once. Table 5 shows their average monthly levels of participation.

**Table 5**
**Level of Participation in the Commercial Gay Scene in an Average Month**

| Type of establishment | Fewer than once or never | 1-4 times | 5-8 times | More than 8 times |
|---|---|---|---|---|
| Gay bars/pubs | 45 (37.8%) | 56 (47.1%) | 13 (10.9%) | 5 (4.2%) |
| Gay baths/saunas | 100 (84.0%) | 17 (14.3%) | 2 (1.7%) | 0 (0.0%) |
| Gay discos | 98 (82.3%) | 20 (16.8%) | 1 (0.9%) | 0 (0.0%) |
| Gay bookstores | 77 (64.7%) | 41 (34.4%) | 1 (0.9%) | 0 (0.0%) |

N= 119

Table 5 indicates that a great majority of the respondents go to these establishments, except for gay bars/pubs, fewer than once a month. Gay bars/pubs are the most frequented establishments, possibly due to their higher availability compared to the other three. The average monthly participation for all of the establishments is 2.1 times for gay bars/pubs, 0.6 time for gay bookstores, and 0.3 time for both gay baths/saunas and gay discos.

## Perceptions of the Commercial Gay Scene

Only a few respondents speak favorably of the commercial gay
scene. The following is the typical response:

> I like the fact that it is totally egalitarian. You can meet peo-
> ple from all walks of life, all kinds of groups, cultural and so-
> cial. It, to me, expresses more the Christian lifestyle than the
> heterosexual world because the barriers are down. People ac-
> cept each other on the basis of their sexuality and not
> whether they are black or white or rich or poor. I think there
> is more harmony. (James, architect, late 40s)

James, who goes with his partner and friends to gay bars/pubs
five times, and gay discos and bookstores at least once in an average
month, highlights the sense of community that the commercial gay
scene offers. It fosters a collective identity of gay people regardless of
their backgrounds.

Simon, a psychotherapist in his late 60s, who goes to the gay
bars/pubs with his partner twice a month, argues that being in the
gay scene is like "swimming in the water where I am familiar."
(Questionnaire data). Similarly, Keith, an unemployed person in his
mid-60s, goes with his partner and mutual friends to the gay
bars/pubs four times, gay discos twice, gay baths/saunas and bookstores once in an average month. He explains metaphorically that the
gay scene is where "people speak the same language." (Questionnaire
data). Elton, in his mid-30s, goes to gay pubs/bars six times and gay
discos once every month with his partner. He says, "The thing I like
about the scene is being able to dance, kiss or cuddle my lover in a
sociable gay atmosphere where we can be out in public and be ourselves and be with friends." (Questionnaire data).

A considerable majority, however, do not perceive the commercial
gay scene in such favorable light. The following are some typical responses:

> The gay scene is very cruel. It is all based on what you look
> like, what you have got in your trousers and how young you
> are. The reason why I don't like going is because you can't ac-
> tually go there and talk to people because people think there
> is a motive behind it. If I had a motive behind it, I probably
> would go because I can pick people up. I think that's ulti-
> mately what it is for. (Jackson, financial professional, late
> 20s)

> The gay scene seems to be more sexual oriented. It is serving
> a certain group of people who didn't want to be attached or

involved and only sees sex as the only thing. (Jimmy, teacher, mid-30s)

I don't like to be "sized up" as potential anything!!! Fleeting acquaintance with the scene makes it seem a bit like a meat-market to me. (Shaun, retired, mid-60s; Questionnaire data)

I feel the lack of love in these places. Unless a person is very outgoing, they can often end up very lonely even though the actual place may be crowded. (Mike, musician, late 40s; Questionnaire data)

These accounts reveal that the commercial gay scene is youth- and physique-oriented. It is also extremely sexual in nature. This perception is resonant with the comment of Philip Blumstein and Pepper Schwartz that, "the problem with the gay male culture is that much of it is organized around singlehood or maintaining one's sexual marketability. Meeting places like bars and baths promote casual sex rather than couple activities." [4]

The above comment is telling. With its considerable emphasis on youth and sex, the commercial gay scene alienates older gay men and those whose sexual needs are met within a partnership. This reflects the situation of many respondents. With an average age of 43.4 and an average length of partnership of 9 years and 5 months (see Appendix), many might think that the commercial gay scene does not hold much attraction for them. Neil (mid-30s) and Damien (mid-50s), who have been together for 14 years and 3 months, illustrate the "age and coupled" factor:

*Neil*: No I am not active in the gay scene. I would say it has got to be because I am in a stable relationship. I used to go out in the beginning because I was looking for a partner or I was looking for somebody for some sort of contact: physical, emotional, whatever. That need is not there anymore. I don't need that whatsoever.

*Damien*: I am old now. You see, the thing about the gay scene is, it is a very young scene now. Men come out much earlier now. There is not the fear. There is not the stigma. A lot of men and boys come out at 17 now and are mixing in the gay scene. So it is a very young scene. I feel I have passed that actually.

It seems that acknowledging the fulfilment of one's needs within a partnership does affect one's desire to participate in the gay scene, particularly when the gay scene is perceived to be unfriendly. Paul (late 20s) and Kieran (late 30s), who have been together for 4 years, lend support to the above argument.

> *Paul*: I think the gay scene is unfriendly. I think you can get a cold shoulder quite easily. It is difficult to talk to people sometimes if you just want to go and talk, because people look at you and then look away. You would feel uncomfortable.

> *Kieran*: I think being in a secure relationship, I don't feel the need of the gay scene. All my needs, emotional, physical, mental and spiritual are being met in my relationship. If I were looking for a boyfriend or looking for sex, then I might go out on the scene.

In sum, the majority of respondents view the commercial gay scene as youth-oriented and a milieu for meeting casual sex partners. This means that an older gay man who is also in a stable partnership might find it quite an alienating place to be. That the commercial gay scene is a place which fosters affirmation to one's sexuality and a collective identity contradicts with the pervasive perception of older gay men. The scene has become a place meant for a particular segment of the gay community who fits the conventional definition of masculinity. Those who do not will experience a sense of internal marginalization in a milieu which is supposedly developed for them. Unfortunately, this kind of marginalization is more detrimental than the external marginalization they might experience in the society at large.

# And Finally . . .

A friend once said that a writer's first book should be about herself or himself. I hope I have not done that in this first book of mine. While I did make it explicit where I was coming from in the Introduction, I have retreated myself to the background after that. I intended this book to be the stories of the gay male Christian couples I studied, a documentation of their love and commitment.

Same-sex relationships are still by and large on the fringe of mainstream sociological discourse and public consciousness. It is a topic about which we have so little knowledge. This is principally an outcome of our culture's tendency to embrace the familiar at the expense of exploring the unfamiliar. We have learned to overcategorize people and oversimplify social life. Sociologists, ironically, are partially responsible for this.

So this book is an attempt to put this topic more central to sociological discourse and public consciousness. It is not an easy task, only because the resistance is colossal. I have highlighted in the Introduction some of my own experiences with this resistance. Even in the sociological community in which I expect broadmindedness to prevail, the ride has not been easy. There is always the need to justify, to fight for the space to be heard and to be taken seriously.

A sociologist who knows quite a lot about my work once said to me, "I do think your work on gay male couples is interesting. But, tell me dear, where is the sociology in it?" Would he have asked the same question if my study were on heterosexual couples? The answer is a definite NO. Operating with the same perception, the editors of a journal once asked me why my article about sexual nonexclusivity in gay male Christian partnerships "is of sociological interest (as distinct from human interest!)?" I found the question understandable, but not excusable. Would I have been asked to justify if the article were about how heterosexual couples managed sexual nonexclusivity? Why should the nature of the relationships determine whether they are sociological or not in empirical research?

What makes the difference? Why should the study of same-sex couples be justified before it can be considered sociological? Surely sociology is not only concerned with the experientially familiar and morally straightforward.

I profoundly believe that it is very important for sociological discourse to provide space for the experiences of minority groups (ethnic, sexual, gender, or others) to be represented *as they are*. I do not think that the validity of same-sex experiences can only be sociologically established when compared to those of heterosexual, the majority, and the perceived norm. Same-sex relationships and "families" are in existence. It is a great shame if sociological discourse does not recognize their existence and continue to confine itself to assumptions based almost exclusively on heterosexual experiences. This scenario calls for a paradigm shift. Indeed, we are in need of a more inclusive paradigm for the study of *human* intimate relationships.

My commitment to this end is clearly demonstrated in my deliberate attempt not to incorporate comparisons with heterosexual partnerships in this book. We simply know too little about same-sex relationships. And the little we know is often colored by some inaccurate assumptions. I do not deny the similarity that exists between same-sex and cross-sex partnerships. However, they also differ in a myriad of significant ways. Let's not over-simplify social life at the expense of diversity. The blind search for universality often impoverishes the richness of human experiences.

I have also deliberately withheld much data about how the gay men I interviewed justify the compatibility between their sexuality and Christian beliefs. Many people are still very interested in this issue. But my respondents, like many other gay men and lesbians, have long moved away from the "right or wrong" or "justification" stage. They have focused their energy on establishing fulfilling life and meaningful social relationships, thus transcending the "deviant" circumstances imposed on them for far too long. They might have once locked themselves in the closet and swallowed the key, as Paul Monette puts it.[1] But now they have freed themselves from this bondage of lonely and soul-wrecking existence. Against all the odds, they have survived and thrived. This is a testimony of human courage and commitment. This deserves respect. This deserves a voice, a listening.

There is a limit as to how much justice a book can do to the life stories of the gay male Christian couples. This book aims only to present a snapshot of the partnerships. They deserve a closer look. They deserve more detailed research. I only hope that even this snapshot can help turn fear to courage, prejudice to understanding, and contempt to respect.

Sometimes, it is not in the clamour of rhetoric and theorizing that we are enlightened. Enlightenment often comes in the silence of the human heart. A silence so profound that it speaks to our human conscience, the element that binds us all together.

Thanks for listening!

# Appendix:
# Research Methodology

The most commonly used research tools in the study of gay male relationships are the questionnaire and the interview.[1] I decided to use both of these research tools for their distinctive strengths. I used postal self-completion questionnaires in order to reach gay male couples in as wide a geographical area as possible. The interview, on the other hand, allowed me to gather a wealth of in-depth data that the former could not possibly do.

A 13-page self-completion questionnaire was posted to all individual respondents with prepaid returned envelopes. The questionnaire contained both open and closed questions eliciting information pertaining to the respondent's biographical data and issues such as living arrangement, leisure activity, domestic division of labor and financial arrangement. Sixty-eight couples (136 individual respondents) completed the questionnaires. I carried out this stage of data collection between March and June 1993.

As soon as the questionnaires from both partners were received, I telephoned the couple to make an appointment for the interview. Using a semi-structured guide, I interviewed the partners separately for about 75 minutes each. This was followed by an interview with the couple together for an average of 30 minutes. The individual interview was designed to collect information pertaining to the respondent's personal experiences and his views on the social, religious, and sexual dimensions of the partnership. Sensitive information such as the respondent's possible sexual encounter outside the partnership was elicited in this interview. I used the couple interview to elicit information about the history of the partnership and the different dimensions of the partnership.

All of the interviews were tape recorded and later transcribed. I interviewed the couples in their homes, except in one case where the interview took place in a private social club of the couple's choice. Time and financial constraints did not allow me to interview all of the 68 couples. I eventually interviewed a subsample of 30 couples who lived primarily in Greater London and the South East of England, where I was then based. I carried out this stage of data collection between April and September 1993.

## CASTING THE NET

The gay population is to a large extent hidden despite the burgeoning commercial gay scene in metropolis such as London and Manchester. Random probability sampling is therefore impracticable.[2] In obtaining an opportunistic sample, personal contacts (e.g., friendship network) and snowballing are the two most commonly used sampling methods in the research on the gay population.[3]

Between November and December 1992, I approached three gay Christian organizations for assistance and fortunately obtained their full support to the study. During February and April 1993, I posted covering letters to all the male members of the Lesbian and Gay Christian Movement (LGCM), QUEST (an organization for Catholic lesbians and gays), and the Anglican Clergy Consultation (ACC). The ACC is a support group for gay priests and their partners in the Church of England. The covering letter, with a response slip attached, provided details about the study and the assurance of confidentiality. All the covering letters were sent out through the organizations, with a note from the chairpersons, calling for support to the study and declaring the assurance of my integrity as a researcher. Some covering letters were also passed to prospective respondents through several personal contacts.

In total, 1301 covering letters were distributed and 222 responses were received. However, as I sent out the covering letters to all the male members of the organizations without knowing their social circumstances, only 71 of the responses met the criteria of the study. Most of the negative responses constituted those who were not in partnership, those in partnerships less than a year, or those with non-Christian partners. Three couples, however, later pulled out of the study, thus the total of 68.

## THE RESPONDENTS

**Table 6**
**Age**

| Age Group | No. of Respondents | Percentage |
|-----------|-------------------|------------|
| 16 to 20 | 1 | 0.7 |
| 21 to 25 | 3 | 2.2 |
| 26 to 30 | 16 | 11.8 |
| 31 to 35 | 23 | 16.9 |
| 36 to 40 | 23 | 16.9 |
| 41 to 45 | 18 | 13.2 |
| 46 to 50 | 16 | 11.8 |
| 51 to 55 | 7 | 5.1 |
| 56 to 60 | 11 | 8.1 |
| 61 to 65 | 13 | 9.6 |
| 66 to 70 | 1 | 0.7 |
| Above 70 | 4 | 3.0 |

N= 136
Mean Age = 43.4 years.
Note: This sample is substantially older than samples of other studies. For example, 33 years (Silverstein, C. 1981. *Man To Man: Gay Couples in America.* New York: William Morrow); 37.5 years (McWhirter, D. P., and A. M. Mattison. 1984. *The Male Couple: How Relationships Develop.* Englewood Cliffs: Prentice-Hall); 35 years (Blasband, D., and L. A. Peplau. 1985. Sexual exclusivity versus openness in gay male couples. *Archives of Sexual Behaviour* 14 (5): 395-412); 32 years (Davies, P. M., F. C. I. Hickson, P. Weatherburn, and A. J. Hunt. 1993. *Sex, Gay Men and AIDS.* London: Falmer Press).

**Table 7**
**Highest Educational Status**

| Highest Educational Level Achieved | No. of Respondents | Percentage |
|-----------|-------------------|------------|
| O-Level | 16 | 11.8 |
| A-Level | 12 | 8.8 |
| First Degree | 55 | 40.4 |
| Master's Degree | 23 | 16.9 |
| Doctoral Degree | 10 | 7.4 |
| Without formal education/ educated under old English or foreign systems | 20 | 14.7 |

N = 136

**Table 8**
**Occupation**

| Occupation | No. of Respondents | Percentage |
|---|---|---|
| Clergy | 29 | 21.3 |
| Teacher/Lecturer | 14 | 10.3 |
| Manager | 9 | 6.7 |
| Administrator | 8 | 5.9 |
| Financial professional | 7 | 5.1 |
| Medical professional | 7 | 5.1 |
| Civil servant | 7 | 5.1 |
| Musician/actor | 6 | 4.4 |
| Computing professional | 3 | 2.2 |
| Social worker | 3 | 2.2 |
| Book/Journal editor | 3 | 2.2 |
| Engineering professional | 2 | 1.5 |
| Stock controller/operator | 2 | 1.5 |
| Book binder/tenor | 2 | 1.5 |
| Clerk | 2 | 1.5 |
| Waiter | 2 | 1.5 |
| Sales executive | 1 | 0.7 |
| Not In Employment | 29 | 21.3 |

N = 136

**Table 9**
**Gross Annual Income**

| Gross Annual Income (£) | No. of Respondents | Percentage |
|---|---|---|
| Less Than 5000 | 17 | 12.5 |
| 5000 --- 8999 | 15 | 11.0 |
| 9000 --- 12999 | 33 | 24.3 |
| 13000 --- 16999 | 28 | 20.6 |
| 17000 --- 20999 | 14 | 10.3 |
| 21000 --- 24999 | 13 | 9.6 |
| 25000 --- 28999 | 7 | 5.1 |
| 29000 --- 32000 | 4 | 2.9 |
| More than 32000 | 5 | 3.7 |

N= 136

**Table 10**
**Religious Affiliation**

| Religious Affiliation | No. of Respondents | Percentage |
|---|---|---|
| Church of England | 82 | 60.3 |
| Roman Catholic | 35 | 25.7 |
| Methodist | 7 | 5.1 |
| Baptist | 3 | 2.2 |
| United Reformed Church | 1 | 0.7 |
| Other | 8 | 6.0 |

N= 136

**Table 11**
**Geographical Distribution**

| Region | No. of Respondents | Percentage |
|---|---|---|
| Greater London | 47 | 34.6 |
| South East | 19 | 13.9 |
| East Anglia | 11 | 8.0 |
| East Midlands | 10 | 7.4 |
| North West | 10 | 7.4 |
| West Midlands | 9 | 6.6 |
| South West | 8 | 5.9 |
| North | 6 | 4.4 |
| Yorkshire and Humberside | 2 | 1.5 |
| Scotland | 10 | 7.4 |
| Wales | 4 | 2.9 |

N= 136

**Table 12**
**Length of Partnership**

| Length of Partnership | No. of Couples | Percentage |
|---|---|---|
| 1 year and up to 3 years | 19 | 28.0 |
| More than 3 years and up to 5 years | 9 | 13.2 |
| More than 5 years and up to 10 years | 13 | 19.1 |
| More than 10 years and up to 15 years | 11 | 16.2 |
| More than 15 years and up to 20 years | 10 | 14.7 |
| Beyond 20 years | 6 | 8.8 |

N= 68
Shortest length of partnership = 1 year
Longest length of partnership = 33 years
Mean length of partnership = 9 years 5 months

Forty couples (67.6%) are cohabiting while 22 couples (32.4%) live apart. For the 30 couples interviewed couples, 20 are cohabiting and 10 live apart. Except one Japanese, one Anglo-Chinese, and one Afro-American, all of the other respondents are white.

With the exception of age, the sample of this study bears great similarity to the samples generally recruited for studies on gay men. Very often, the sample overrepresents the young, middle- and upper-middle class, educated whites living in urban areas.[4] Therefore, the findings of this study should not be overgeneralized. Nonetheless, they throw light on the dynamics of gay male Christian partnerships.

# Notes

## INTRODUCTION

1. Peck, S. 1993. *Further Along the Road Less Traveled: The Unending Journey towards Spiritual Growth*. London: Simon & Schuster, p. 107. Peck also argues that a myriad of factors determine the aetiology of homosexuality, including God's creation, p. 104-105.

2. Yip, A. K. T. 1995. *Dynamics of Gay Christian Partnerships*. Unpublished PhD Thesis, University of Surrey, Guildford, UK.

3. Yip, A. K. T. 1995. Gay does not mean ungodly. *The Sunday Times*, 20 August.

4. See, for example, Berzon, B., and R. Leighton. 1979. *Positively Gay*. Millbrae: Celestial Arts; Marcus, E. 1988. *The Male Couple's Guide to Living Together*. New York: Harper & Row; Berzon, B. 1989. *Permanent Partners: Building Gay and Lesbian Relationships that Last*. New York: Penguin; Tessina, T. 1989. *Gay Relationships for Men and Women*. Los Angeles: Jeremy R. Tarcher; Driggs, J. H., and S. E. Finn. 1990. *Intimacy Between Men: How to Find and Keep Gay Love Relationships*. New York: Plume; Sanderson, T. 1990. *Making Gay Relationships Work: A Handbook for Male Couples*. London: The Other Way Press.

5. See the list of my publications in the Bibliography.

6. De Cecco, J. P. 1988. *Gay Relationships*. New York: Harrington Park Press, p.3.

7. For a detailed discussion see Baxter, L. A. 1993. The social side of personal relationships: A dialectical perspective. In *Social Context and Relationships*, ed. S. Duck, 135-165. London: Sage.

## CHAPTER 1
## THE BEGINNING PERIOD

1. Bell, A. P., and M. S. Weinberg. 1978. *Homosexualities: A Study of Diversity among Men and Women.* New York: Simon and Schuster; See also Huston, M., and P. Schwartz. 1996. Gendered dynamics in the romantic relationships of lesbians and gay men. In *Gendered Relationships*, ed. J. T. Wood, 163-176. Moutain View, CA: Mayfield.

2. Peplau, L. A., and S. D. Cochran. 1981. Value orientations in the intimate relationships of gay men. *Journal of Homosexuality* 6 (3): 1-19.

3. See, for example, Klinkenberg, D., and S. Rose. 1994. Dating scripts of gay men and lesbians. *Journal of Homosexuality* 26 (4): 23-35.

4. Weinberg, M. S., and C. J. Williams. 1974. *Male Homosexuals: Their Problems and Adaptations.* New York: Penguin.

5. Giddens, A. 1991. *Modernity and Self-Identity: Self and Society in the Late Modern Age.* Cambridge: Polity Press.

6. This is contradictory to Raymond Berger's findings. He reports that 62% of the 92 gay male couples he studied favor *lover*. Only 22.5% prefer *partner*. Similarly, Steve Bryant and Demian report that among the 560 gay male couples they studied, 40% prefer *lover* and 27% partner/life partner. See Berger, R. M. 1990. Men together: Understanding the gay couple. *Journal of Homosexuality* 19 (3): 31-49; and Bryant, A. S., and Demian. 1994. Relationship characteristics of American gay and lesbian couples: Findings from a national survey. *Journal of Gay and Lesbian Social Services* 1: 101-117.

7. See, for example, arguments put forward by Wolfson, E. 1996. Why we should fight for the freedom to marry: The challenges and opportunities that will follow a win in Hawaii. *Journal of Gay, Lesbian and Bisexual Identity* 1 (1): 79-89. For a more general discussion of the issue, see also Sullivan, A. 1995. *Virtually Normal: An Argument about Homosexuality.* New York: Picador; Eskridge, W. N. Jr. 1996. *From Sexual Liberty to Civilized Commitment: The Case for Same-Sex Marriage.* New York: The Free Press; and Sherman, S. ed. 1996. *Lesbian and Gay Marriage.* Philadelphia: Temple University Press.

8. See, for example, arguments put forward by Brownworth, V. A. 1996. Tying the knot or the hangman's noose: The case against marriage. *Journal of Gay, Lesbian and Bisexual Identity* 1 (1): 91-98. For a more general discussion of the issue, see also Eskridge, W. N. Jr. 1996. *From Sexual Liberty to Civilized Commitment: The Case for Same-Sex Marriage.* New York: The Free Press; and Sherman, S. ed. 1996. *Lesbian and Gay Marriage.* Philadelphia: Temple University Press.

## CHAPTER 2
## LEARNING TO SHARE LIFE TOGETHER

1. They propose a six-stage developmental model for gay male partnerships. See McWhirter, D. P., and A. M. Mattison. 1984. *The Male Couple: How Relationships Develop.* Englewood Cliffs: Prentice-Hall.

2. Kurdek, L. A. 1993. The allocation of household labor in gay, lesbian, and heterosexual married couples. *Journal of Social Issues* 49: 127-140.

3. McWhirter, D. P., and A. M. Mattison. 1984. *The Male Couple: How Relationships Develop.* Englewood Cliffs: Prentice-Hall.

4. Egalitarianism is a prominent characteristic of gay male partnerships. See, for example, Peplau, L. A. 1981. What homosexuals want in relationships. *Psychology Today* 15 (March): 28-38; Kurdek, L. A. 1993. The allocation of household labor in gay, lesbian, and heterosexual married couples. *Journal of Social Issues* 49: 127-140.

5. See, for example, Driggs, J. H., and S. E. Finn. 1990. *Intimacy Between Men: How to Find and Keep Gay Love Relationships.* New York: Plume; Wood, J. T. 1994. Gender and relationship crises: Contrasting reasons, responses, and relational orientations. In *Queer Words, Queer Images: Communication of Homosexuality*, ed. R. J. Ringer, 238-264. New York: New York University Press.


CHAPTER 3
WAR AND PEACE: MANAGING CONFLICT

1. Kurdek, L. A. 1991. Correlates of relationship satisfaction in cohabiting gay and lesbian couples: Integration of contextual, investment, and problem-solving models. *Journal of Personality and Social Psychology* 61: 910-922; Kurdek, L. A. 1994. Conflict resolution styles in gay, lesbian, heterosexual nonparent and heterosexual parent couples. *Journal of Marriage and the Family* 56 (August): 705-722.

2. For a detailed discussion, see Baxter, L. A. 1993. The social side of personal relationships: A dialectical perspective. In *Social Context and Relationships*, ed. S. Duck, 135-165. London: Sage; Baxter, L. A. 1994. A dialogic approach to relationship maintenance. In *Understanding Personal Relationships*, eds. D. J. Canary and L. Stafford, 243-265. London: Sage; Yip, A. K. T. 1995. *Dynamics of Gay Christian Partnerships.* Unpublished PhD Thesis, University of Surrey, Guildford, UK, Chapter 1.

3. This is one of the main areas of conflict in both same-sex and cross-sex intimate relationships. See Bryant, A. S., and Demian. 1994. Relationship characteristics of American gay and lesbian couples: Findings from a national survey. *Journal of Gay and Lesbian Social Services* 1: 101-117; Kurdek, L. A. 1994. Areas of conflict for gay, lesbian and heterosexual couples: What couples argue about influence relationship satisfaction. *Journal of Marriage and the Family* 56 (November): 923-934; Wood, J. T. 1994. Gender and relationship crises: Contrasting reasons, responses, and relational orientations. In *Queer Words, Queer Images: Communication of Homosexuality*, ed. R. J. Ringer, 238-264. New York: New York University Press.

4. An individual's perception of his or her investment size (e.g., in terms of resources, time, emotional energy) in comparison to that of his or her partner determines the level of relationship satisfaction. See, for example, Duffy, S. M., and C. E. Rusbult. 1986. Satisfaction and commitment in homosexual and heterosexual relationships. *Journal of Homosexuality* 12 (2): 1-23; Kurdek, L. A. 1992. Relationship stability and rela-

tionship satisfaction in cohabiting gay and lesbian couples: A Prospective longitudinal test of the contextual and interdependence models. *Journal of Social and Personal Relationships* 9: 125-142; Kurdek, L. A. 1994. The nature or correlates of relationship quality in gay, lesbian, and heterosexual cohabiting couples: A test of the individual difference, interdependence, and discrepancy models. *In Lesbian and Gay Psychology: Theory, Research, and Clinical Applications*, eds. B. Greene and G. M. Herek, 133-155. London: Sage.

5. This is widely acknowledged in research on cross-sex and same-sex couples. The differences between these couples, however, should not be overlooked. See, for example, Askham, J. 1984. *Identity and Stability in Marriage*. Cambridge: Cambridge University Press; Finch, J., and D. Morgan. 1991. Marriage in the 1990s: A new sense of realism? In *Marriage, Domestic Life and Social Change: Writings for Jacqueline Burgoyne*, ed. D. Clark, 55-80. London: Routledge; De Cecco, J. P. 1988. *Gay Relationships*. New York: Harrington Park Press.

6. For example, McWhirter, D. P., and A. M. Mattison. 1984. *The Male Couple: How Relationships Develop*. Englewood Cliffs: Prentice-Hall.

7. Rusbult, C. E. 1987. Responses to dissatisfaction in close relationships: The exit-voice-loyalty-neglect model. In *Intimate Relationships: Development, Dynamics, Deterioration*, eds. D. Perlman and S. W. Duck, 209-237. London: Sage.

8. Kurdek, L. A. 1991. The dissolution of gay and lesbian couples. *Journal of Social and Personal Relationships* 8 (2): 265-278.

9. Modrcin, M. J., and N. L. Wyers. 1990. Lesbian and gay couples: Where they turn when help is needed. *Journal of Gay and Lesbian Psychotherapy* 1 (3): 89-104.

10. Blumstein, P., and P. Schwartz. 1983. *American Couples: Money, Work, Sex*. New York: Simon & Schuster; Lee, J. A. 1990. Can we talk? Can we really talk?: Communication as a key factor in the maturing homosexual couple. *Journal of Homosexuality* 20 (3/4): 143-168; Duck, S. 1994. Steady as (s)he goes: Relational maintenance as a shared meaning system. In *Communication and Relational Maintenance*, eds. D. J. Canary and L. Stafford, 45-60. New York: Academic Press.

11. De Cecco, J. P., and M. G. Shively. 1978. A study of perceptions of rights and needs in interpersonal conflicts in homosexual relationships. *Journal of Homosexuality* 3 (3): 205-216; Klein, R. C. A., and H. Lamm. 1996. Legitimate interest in couple conflict. *Journal of Social and Personal Relationships* 13 (4): 619-626.

12. Baucom, D. H. 1987. Attributes in distressed relations: How can we explain them? In *Intimate Relationships: Development, Dynamics, Deterioration*, eds. D. Perlman and S. W. Duck, 177-206. London: Sage, p. 184.

13. Duck, S., and M. Lea. 1983. Breakdown of personal relationships and the threat to personal identity. In *Threatened Identities*, ed. G. M. Breakwell, 53-73. Chichester, UK: John Wiley & Sons.

14. Research evidence suggests that most gay male partnerships operate within a "best friend" model, emphasizing the ethic of equality and reciprocity. See, for example, Peplau, L. A., and S. L. Gordon. 1983. The intimate relationships of lesbians and gay men. In *Changing Boundaries: Gender Roles and Sexual Behavior*, eds. E. R. Allgeier and N. B. McCormick, 226-244. Palo Alto, CA: Mayfield; Kurdek, L. A., and J. P. Schmitt.

1987. Partner homogamy in married, heterosexual cohabiting, gay, and lesbian couples. *Journal of Sex Research* 23: 212-232.

15. Giddens, A. 1991. *Modernity and Self-Identity: Self and Society in the Late Modern Age*. Cambridge: Polity Press; Giddens, A. 1992. *The Transformation of Intimacy*. Cambridge: Polity Press; Weeks, J. 1995. *Invented Moralities*. Cambridge: Polity Press.

## CHAPTER 4
## WHAT IS YOURS IS MINE, WHAT IS MINE IS OURS?: FINANCIAL ARRANGEMENTS

1. Blumstein, P., and P. Schwartz. 1983. *American Couples: Money, Work, Sex*. New York: Simon & Schuster, p. 127; See also Harry, J. 1983. Gay male and lesbian couples. In *Contemporary Families and Alternative Lifestyles*, eds. E. D. Macklin and R. H. Robin, 216-234. Beverly Hills, CA: Sage; Huston, M., and P. Schwartz. 1995. The relationships of lesbians and gay men. In *Under-studied Relationships: Off the Beaten Track*, eds. J. T. Wood and S. Duck, 89-121. Thousands Oaks: Sage.

2. Berzon, B., and R. Leighton. 1979. *Positively Gay*. Millbrae: Celestial Arts; Risman, B., and P. Schwartz. 1988. Sociological research on male and female homosexuality. *Annual Review of Sociology* 14: 125-147; Driggs, J. H., and S. E. Finn. 1990. *Intimacy Between Men: How to Find and Keep Gay Love Relationships*. New York: Plume.

3. Conversely, a survey of 560 gay male couples in the United States reports that only 18% of the couples keep finances completely separate. The other 82% either share all or part of their incomes. See Bryant, A. S., and Demian. 1994. Relationship characteristics of American gay and lesbian couples: Findings from a national survey. *Journal of Gay and Lesbian Social Services* 1: 101-117.

4. Blumstein, P., and P. Schwartz. 1983. *American Couples: Money, Work, Sex*. New York: Simon and Schuster, p. 55; See also Harry, J., and W. B. DeVall. 1978. *The Social Organization of Gay Males*. New York: Praeger; Huston, M., and P. Schwartz. 1996. Gendered dynamics in the romantic relationships of lesbians and gay men. In *Gendered Relationships*, ed. J. T. Wood, 163-176. Moutain View, CA: Mayfield.

## CHAPTER 5
## THE "S" FACTOR: SEX

1. Blumstein, P., and P. Schwartz. 1983. *American Couples: Money, Work, Sex*. New York: Simon & Schuster, p. 195.

2. Silverstein, C. 1981. *Man to Man: Gay Couples in America*. New York: William Marrow.

3. See, for example, McWhirter, D. P., and A. M. Mattison. 1984. *The Male Couple: How Relationships Develop*. Englewood Cliffs: Prentice-Hall.

4. For a more detailed discussion on sexual satisfaction in gay partnerships, see Deenen, A. A., L. Gijs, and A. X. Van Naerssen. 1994. In-

timacy and sexuality in gay male couples. *Archives of Sexual Behavior* 23 (4): 421-431.

5. For a more detailed discussion, see Larson, P. C. 1982. Gay male relationships. In *Homosexuality: Social, Psychological and Biological Issues*, eds. W. Paul, J. D. Weinrich, J. C. Gonsiorek, and M. E. Hotvedt, 219-232. Beverly Hills, CA: Sage.

6. See, for example, Saghir, M., and E. Robins. 1973. *Male and Female Homosexuality: A Comprehensive Investigation*. Baltimore: Williams and Wilkins; Harry, J., and W. B. DeVall. 1978. *The Social Organization of Gay Males*. New York: Praeger; Weatherburn, P. 1992. *The Relationship Between the Sexual Behaviour of Homosexually Active Men and Their Age and Relationship Types*. London: Project SIGMA, Paper No. 28; Johnson, A. M., J. Wadsworth, K. Wellings, J. Field, and S. Bradshaw. 1994. *Sexual Behaviour in Britain: The National Survey of Sexual Attitudes and Lifestyles*. West Drayton: Penguin.

7. Harry, J. 1976. On the validity of typologies of gay males. *Journal of Homosexuality* 2 (2): 143-152, p. 149.

8. It is heartening to see that researchers are beginning to recognize this, thus studying sexual techniques as merely activities or acts without locating them within the active-passive model. See, for example, Johnson, A. M., J. Wadsworth, K. Wellings, J. Field, and S. Bradshaw. 1994. *Sexual Behaviour in Britain: The National Survey of Sexual Attitudes and Lifestyles*. West Drayton: Penguin.

9. I am grateful to Project SIGMA (which research into the sexual behavior of men who have sex with men) for allowing me to refer to their *Sex Inventory* in the *SIGMA Question Schedule* (particularly the 1 October 1987 version), on which Table 4 is based.

10. This is consistent with the findings of other studies, for example, Saghir, M., and E. Robins. 1973. *Male and Female Homosexuality: A Comprehensive Investigation*. Baltimore: Williams and Wilkins; Harry, J., and W.B. DeVall. 1978. *The Social Organization of Gay Males*. New York: Praeger.

11. Harry, J. 1976. On the validity of typologies of gay males. *Journal of Homosexuality* 2 (2): 143-152, p. 151.

12. Ellison, M. M. 1994. Common decency: A new Christian sexual ethics. In *Sexuality and the Sacred: Sources for Theological Reflection*, eds. J. B. Nelson and S. P. Longfellow, 236-241. Westminster: John Knox Press, p. 239.

13. See, for example, Nanda, S., and J. S. Francher. 1980. Culture and homosexuality: A comparison of long term gay male and lesbian relationships. *The Eastern Anthropologist* 33: 139-152. Silverstein, C. 1981. *Man To Man: Gay Couples in America*. New York: William Morrow; McWhirter, D. P., and A. M. Mattison. 1984. *The Male Couple: How Relationships Develop*. Englewood Cliffs: Prentice-Hall; Kurdek, L. A. 1991. The dissolution of gay and lesbian couples. *Journal of Social and Personal Relationships* 8 (2): 265-278.

14. Blumstein, P., and P. Schwartz. 1983. *American Couples: Money, Work, Sex*. New York: Simon and Schuster, p. 286. See also Blasband, D., and L. A. Peplau. 1985. Sexual exclusivity versus openness in gay male couples. *Archives of Sexual Behavior* 14 (5): 395-412; Buunk, B. P., and B. Van Driel. 1989. *Variant Lifestyles and Relationships*. Newbury Park:

Sage; Davies, P. M., F. C. I. Hickson, P. Weatherburn, and A. J. Hunt. 1993. *Sex, Gay Men and AIDS*. London: Falmer Press.

15. Hickson, F. C. I. 1991. *Sexual Exclusivity, Non-exclusivity and HIV*. London: Project SIGMA Working, Paper No. 13; Yip, A. K. T. Forthcoming. Gay male Christian couples and sexual exclusivity. *Sociology*.

16. This is also reported by other researchers, for instance, McWhirter, D. P., and A. M. Mattison. 1984. *The Male Couple: How Relationships Develop*. Englewood Cliffs: Prentice-Hall; Blasband, D., and L. A. Peplau. 1985. Sexual exclusivity versus openness in gay male couples. *Archives of Sexual Behavior* 14 (5): 395-412.

17. For a more detailed discussion on this concept, see Lyons, R. F., and D. Meade. 1995. Painting a new face on relationships: Relationship remodeling in response to chronic illness. In *Confronting Relationship Challenges*, eds. S. Duck and J. T. Wood, 181-210. Thousand Oaks, CA: Sage.

18. Blasband, D., and L. A. Peplau. 1985. Sexual exclusivity versus openness in gay male couples. *Archives of Sexual Behavior* 14 (5): 395-412, p. 411.

19. Harry, J., and W.B. DeVall. 1978. *The Social Organization of Gay Males*. New York: Praeger.

## CHAPTER 6
## SPIRITUALITY AND SEXUALITY: MANAGING A CHRISTIAN FAITH

1. I have addressed this issue elsewhere. See my publications: Attacking the attacker: Gay Christians talk back. *British Journal of Sociology*; and The politics of counter-rejection: Gay Christians and the church. *Journal of Homosexuality*.

2. Greenberg, J. S. 1973. A study of the self-esteem and alienation of male homosexuals. *Journal of Psychology* 83: 137-143; Weinberg, M. S., and C. J. Williams. 1974. *Male Homosexuals: Their Problems and Adaptations*. New York: Penguin; Gonsiorek, J. 1988. Mental health issues of gay and lesbian adolescents. *Journal of Adolescent Health Care* 9: 114-122; Wagner, G., J. Serafini, J. Rabkin, R. Remien, and J. Williams. 1994. Integration of one's religion and homosexuality: A weapon against internalized homophobia? *Journal of Homosexuality* 26 (4): 91-110.

3. For detailed discussions on gay identity development, see Cass, V. C. 1979. Homosexual identity formation: A theoretical model. *Journal of Homosexuality* 4 (3): 219-235; Plummer, K. 1975. *Sexual Stigma: An Interactionist Account*. London: Routledge & Kegan Paul; Troiden, R. R. 1979. Becoming homosexual: A model of gay identity acquisition. *Psychiatry: Journal for the Study of Interpersonal Processes* 42: 362-373; Troiden, R. R. 1984. Self, self-concept, identity, and homosexual identity: Constructs in need of definition and differentiation. *Journal of Homosexuality* 10 (3&4): 97-107; Thumma, S. 1991. Negotiating a religious identity: The case of the gay evangelical. *Sociological Analysis* 52 (4): 333-347; Eliason, M. J. 1996a. An inclusive model of lesbian identity assumption. *Journal of Gay, Lesbian, and Bisexual Identity* 1 (1): 3-19. For a good literature

review of this issue, see Eliason, M. J. 1996b. Identity formation for lesbian, bisexual, and gay persons: Beyond a "minoritizing" view. *Journal of
Homosexuality* 30 (3): 31-58.

4. The Church of England in general considers same-sex genital acts
as falling short of the ideal of heterosexual marriage; see Church of England. 1987. *General Synod Report of Proceedings (Volume 18)*. London:
CIO; Church of England. 1991. *Issues in Human Sexuality: A Statement
by the House of Bishops*. London: Church House Publishing. The Roman
Catholic Church labels the homosexual orientation an "objective disorder" and same-sex genital acts "intrinsically disordered", see Congregation for the Doctrine of the Faith. 1986. *Letter to the Bishops of the
Catholic Church on the Pastoral Care of Homosexual Persons*. London:
Catholic Truth Society; Hume, B. 1993. Cardinal Hume's observations
on the Catholic Church's teaching concerning homosexual people. *Briefing* 22 July: 4-5; Hume, B. 1995. A note on the teaching of the Catholic
Church concerning homosexual people. *Briefing* 16 March: 3-5. For a
general discussion on the stances adopted by various major institutional-
ized churches, see Brash, A. A. 1995. *Facing Our Differences: The
Churches and Their Gay and Lesbian Members*. Geneva: World Council of
Churches; Hertman, K. 1996. *Congregations in Conflict: The Battle Over
Homosexuality*. New Brunswick, NJ: Rutgers University Press.

5. There is a great wealth of theological literature on this issue. See,
for example Boswell, J. 1980. *Christianity, Social Tolerance and Homo-
sexuality*. Chicago: University of Chicago Press; McNeill, J. J. 1988. *The
Church and the Homosexual*. Boston: Beacon Press; Coleman, P. 1989.
*Gay Christian: A Moral Dilemma*. London: SCM Press; John, J. 1993.
*Permanent, Faithful, Stable: Christian Same-Sex Partnerships*. London:
Affirming Catholicism; Seow, C. L. 1996. *Homosexuality and Christian
Community*. Louisville, Ky: Westminster John Knox Press; Stuart, E.,
and A. Thatcher. 1996. *Christian Perspectives on Sexuality and Gender*.
Leominster, UK: Gracewing; Vasey, M. 1996. *Friends and Strangers: A
New Exploration of Homosexuality and the Bible*. London: Hodder &
Stoughton.

6. Hanningan, J. A. 1993. New social movement theory and the soci-
ology of religion: Synergies and syntheses. In *A Future for Religion?: New
Paradigms for Social Analysis*, ed. W. H. Jr. Swatos, 1-18. Newbury Park,
CA: Sage.

## CHAPTER 7
## NETWORKING: PARTICIPATION IN THE
## GAY SUBCULTURE

1. Lyman, S. M. 1970. *The Asian in the West*. Reno and Las Vegas:
Western Studies Center, Desert Research Institute.

2. For a review of the debate on assimilationism, see Manning, T.
1995. Assimilationism: Are you guilty or not guilty. *Gay Times* April: 19-
24.

3. These are often termed the "instrumental" and the "expressive"
natures of participation in identity politics or social movements. See Gusfield, J. R. 1963. *Symbolic Crusade: Status Politics and the American*

*Temperance Movement.* Urbana: University of Illinois Press; Parkin, F. 1968. *Middle Class Radicalism: The Social Bases of the British Campaign for Nuclear Disarmament.* Manchester: Manchester University Press.

    4. Blumstein, P., and P. Schwartz. 1983. *American Couples: Money, Work, Sex.* New York: Simon & Schuster, p. 322.


## AND FINALLY

    1. Monette, P. 1994. *Becoming a Man: Half a Life Story.* London: Abacus.


## APPENDIX

    1. See my literature review in Yip, A. K. T. 1995. *Dynamics of Gay Christian Partnerships.* Unpublished PhD Thesis, University of Surrey, Guildford, UK, Chapter 2.
    2. Morin, S. F. 1977. Heterosexual bias in psychological research on lesbianism and male homosexuality. *American Psychologist* 32 (8): 629-637; Peplau, L. A. 1981. What homosexuals want in relationships. *Psychology Today* 15 (March): 28-38.
    3. See my literature review in Yip, A. K. T. 1995. *Dynamics of Gay Christian Partnerships.* Unpublished PhD Thesis, University of Surrey, Guildford, UK, Chapter 2.
    4. See, for example, Silverstein, C. 1981. *Man to Man: Gay Couples in America.* New York: William Morrow; Peplau, L. A. 1982. Research on homosexual couples: An overview. *Journal of Homosexuality* 8 (2): 3-8; McWhirter, D. P., and A. M. Mattison. 1984. *The Male Couple: How Relationships Develop.* Englewood Cliffs: Prentice-Hall; Berger, R. M. 1990. Men together: Understanding the gay couple. *Journal of Homosexuality* 19 (3): 31-49; Meyer, J. 1990. Guess who's coming to dinner this time? A study of gay intimate relationships and the support for these relationships. *Marriage and Family Review* 14 (3/4): 59-82; Kurdek, L. A. 1992. Relationship stability and relationship satisfaction in cohabiting gay and lesbian couples: A prospective longitudinal test of the contextual and interdependence models. *Journal of Social and Personal Relationships* 9 (1): 125-142; Bryant, A. S., and Demian. 1994. Relationship characteristics of American gay and lesbian couples: Findings from a national survey. *Journal of Gay and Lesbian Social Services* 1 (2): 101-117.

# Bibliography

Askham, J. 1984. *Identity and Stability in Marriage*. Cambridge: Cambridge University Press.

Baucom, D. H. 1987. Attributes in distressed relations: How can we explain them? In *Intimate Relationships: Development, Dynamics, Deterioration*, eds. D. Perlman and S. W. Duck, 177-206. London: Sage.

Baxter, L. A. 1993. The social side of personal relationships: A dialectical perspective. In *Social Context and Relationships*, ed. S. Duck, 135-165. London: Sage.

Baxter, L. A. 1994. A dialogic approach to relationship maintenance. In *Understanding Personal Relationships*, eds. D. J. Canary and L. Stafford, 243-265. London: Sage.

Bell, A. P., and M. S. Weinberg. 1978. *Homosexualities: A Study of Diversity among Men and Women*. New York: Simon & Schuster.

Berger, R. M. 1990. Men together: Understanding the gay couple. *Journal of Homosexuality* 19 (3): 31-49.

Berzon, B. 1989. *Permanent Partners: Building Gay and Lesbian Relationships that Last*. New York: Penguin.

Berzon, B., and R. Leighton. 1979. *Positively Gay*. Millbrae: Celestial Arts.

Blasband, D., and L. A. Peplau. 1985. Sexual exclusivity versus openness in gay male couples. *Archives of Sexual Behaviour* 14 (5): 395-412.

Boswell, J. 1980. *Christianity, Social Tolerance and Homosexuality*. Chicago: University of Chicago Press.

Brash, A. A. 1995. *Facing Our Differences: The Churches and Their Gay and Lesbian Members*. Geneva: World Council of Churches.

Brownworth, V. A. 1996. Tying the knot or the hangman's noose: The case against marriage. *Journal of Gay, Lesbian and Bisexual Identity* 1 (1): 91-98.

Bryant, A. S., and Demian. 1994. Relationship characteristics of American gay and lesbian couples: Findings from a national survey. *Journal of Gay and Lesbian Social Services* 1: 101-117.

Buunk, B. P., and B. Van Driel. 1989. *Variant Lifestyles and Relationships*. Newbury Park, CA: Sage.

Cass, V. C. 1979. Homosexual identity formation: A theoretical model. *Journal of Homosexuality* 4 (3): 219-235.

Church of England. 1987. *General Synod Report of Proceedings (Volume 18)*. London: CIO.

Church of England. 1991. *Issues in Human Sexuality: A Statement by the House of Bishops*. London: Church House Publishing.

Coleman, P. *Gay Christian: A Moral Dilemma*. London: SCM Press.

Congregation for the Doctrine of the Faith. 1986. *Letter to the Bishops of the Catholic Church on the Pastoral Care of Homosexual Persons*. London: Catholic Truth Society.

Davies, P. M., F. C. I. Hickson, P. Weatherburn, and A. J. Hunt. 1993. *Sex, Gay Men and AIDS*. London: Falmer Press.

De Cecco, J. P. 1988. *Gay Relationships*. New York: Harrington Park Press.

De Cecco, J. P., and M. G. Shively. 1978. A study of perceptions of rights and needs in interpersonal conflicts in homosexual relationships. *Journal of Homosexuality* 3 (3): 205-216.

Deenen, A. A., L. Gijs, and A. X. Van Naerssen. 1994. Intimacy and sexuality in gay male couples. *Archives of Sexual Behavior* 23 (4): 421-431.

Driggs, J. H., and S. E. Finn. 1990. *Intimacy Between Men: How to Find and Keep Gay Love Relationships*. New York: Plume.

Duck, S., and M. Lea. 1983. Breakdown of personal relationships and the threat to personal identity. In *Threatened Identities*, ed. G. M. Breakwell, 53-73. Chichester, UK: John Wiley & Sons.

Duck, S. 1994. Steady as (s)he goes: Relational maintenance as a shared meaning system. In *Communication and Relational Maintenance*, eds. D. J. Canary and L. Stafford, 45-60. New York: Academic Press.

Duffy, S. M., and C. E. Rusbult. 1986. Satisfaction and commitment in homosexual and heterosexual relationships. *Journal of Homosexuality* 12 (2): 1-23.

Eliason, M. J. 1996a. An inclusive model of lesbian identity assumption. *Journal of Lesbian, Gay, and Bisexual Identity* 1 (1): 3-19.

Eliason, M. J. 1996b. Identity formation for lesbian, bisexual, and gay persons: Beyond a "minoritizing" view. *Journal of Homosexuality* 30 (3): 31-58.

Ellison, M. M. 1994. Common decency: A new Christian sexual ethics. In *Sexuality and the Sacred: Sources for Theological Reflection*, eds. J. B. Nelson and S. P. Longfellow, 236-241. Louisville, Ky: Westminster John Knox Press.

Eskridge, W. N. Jr. 1996. *From Sexual Liberty to Civilized Commitment: The Case for Same-Sex Marriage*. New York: The Free Press.

Finch, J., and D. Morgan. 1991. Marriage in the 1990s: A new sense of realism? In *Marriage, Domestic Life and Social Change: Writings for Jacqueline Burgoyne*, ed. D. Clark. London: Routledge.

Giddens, A. 1991. *Modernity and Self-Identity: Self and Society in the Late Modern Age.* Cambridge: Polity Press.

Giddens, A. 1992. *The Transformation of Intimacy.* Cambridge: Polity Press.

Gonsiorek, J. 1988. Mental health issues of gay and lesbian adolescents. *Journal of Adolescent Health Care* 9: 114-122.

Greenberg, J. S. 1973. A study of the self-esteem and alienation of male homosexuals. *Journal of Psychology* 83: 137-143

Gusfield, J. R. 1963. *Symbolic Crusade: Status Politics and the American Temperance Movement.* Urbana: University of Illinois Press.

Hanningan, J. A. 1993. New social movement theory and the sociology of religion: Synergies and syntheses. In *A Future for Religion?: New Paradigms for Social Analysis,* ed. W. H. Jr. Swatos, 1-18. Newbury Park, CA: Sage.

Harry, J. 1976. On the validity of typologies of gay males. *Journal of Homosexuality* 2 (2): 143-152.

Harry, J. 1983. Gay male and lesbian couples. In *Contemporary Families and Alternative Lifestyles,* eds. E. D. Macklin and R. H. Robin, 216-234. Beverly Hills, CA: Sage.

Harry, J., and W. B. DeVall. 1978. *The Social Organization of Gay Males.* New York: Praeger.

Hertman, K. 1996. *Congregation in Conflict: The Battle Over Homosexuality.* New Brunswick, NJ: Rutgers University Press.

Hickson, F. C. I. 1991. *Sexual Exclusivity, Non-exclusivity and HIV.* London: Project SIGMA, Working Paper No. 13.

Hume, B. 1993. Cardinal Hume's observations on the Catholic Church's teaching concerning homosexual people. *Briefing* 22 July: 4-5.

Hume, B. 1995. A note on the teaching of the Catholic Church concerning homosexual people. *Briefing* 16 March: 3-5.

Huston, M., and P. Schwartz. 1995. The relationships of lesbians and gay men. In *Under-studied Relationships: Off the Beaten Track,* eds. J. T. Wood and S. Duck, 89-121. Thousands Oaks, CA: Sage.

Huston, M., and P. Schwartz. 1996. Gendered dynamics in the romantic relationships of lesbians and gay men. In *Gendered Relationships,* ed. J. T. Wood, 163-176. Mountain View, CA: Mayfield.

John, J. 1993. *Permanent, Faithful, Stable: Christian Same-Sex Partnerships.* London: Affirming Catholicism.

Johnson, A. M., J. Wadsworth, K. Wellings, J. Field, and S. Bradshaw. 1994. *Sexual Behaviour in Britain: The National Survey of Sexual Attitudes and Lifestyles.* West Drayton: Penguin.

Klinkenberg, D., and S. Rose. 1994. Dating scripts of gay men and lesbians. *Journal of Homosexuality* 26 (4): 23-35.

Kurdek, L. A. 1991a. Correlates of relationship satisfaction in cohabiting gay and lesbian couples: Integration of contextual, investment, and problem-solving models. *Journal of Personality and Social Psychology* 61: 910-922.

Kurdek, L. A. 1991b. The dissolution of gay and lesbian couples. *Journal of Social and Personal Relationships* 8 (2): 265-278.

Kurdek, L. A. 1992. Relationship stability and relationship satisfaction in cohabiting gay and lesbian couples: A Prospective longitudinal test of the contextual and interdependence models. *Journal of Social and Personal Relationships* 9: 125-142.

Kurdek, L. A. 1993. The allocation of household labor in gay, lesbian, and heterosexual married couples. *Journal of Social Issues* 49: 127-140.

Kurdek, L. A. 1994a. Conflict resolution styles in gay, lesbian, heterosexual nonparent and heterosexual parent couples. *Journal of Marriage and the Family* 56 (August): 705-722.

Kurdek, L. A. 1994b. The nature or correlates of relationship quality in gay, lesbian, and heterosexual cohabiting couples: A test of the individual difference, interdependence, and discrepancy models. In *Lesbian and Gay Psychology: Theory, Research, and Clinical Applications*, eds. B. Greene and G. M. Herek, 133-155. London: Sage.

Kurdek, L. A. 1994c. Areas of conflict for gay, lesbian and heterosexual couples: What couples argue about influence relationship satisfaction. *Journal of Marriage and the Family* 56 (November): 923-934.

Kurdek, L. A., and J. P. Schmitt. 1987. Partner homogamy in married, heterosexual cohabiting, gay, and lesbian couples. *Journal of Sex Research* 23: 212-232.

Larson, P. C. 1982. Gay male relationships. In *Homosexuality: Social, and Biological Issues*, eds. W. Paul, J. D. Weinrich, J. C. Gonsiorek, and M. E. Hotvedt, 219-232. Beverly Hills, CA: Sage.

Lee, J. A. 1990. Can we talk? Can we really talk?: Communication as a key factor in the maturing homosexual couple. *Journal of Homosexuality* 20 (3/4): 143-168.

Lein, R. C. A., and H. Lamm. 1996. Legitimate interest in couple conflict. *Journal of Social and Personal Relationships* 13 (4): 619-626.

Lyman, S. M. 1970. *The Asian in the West*. Reno and Las Vegas: Western Studies Center, Desert Research Institute.

Lyons, R. F., and D. Meade. 1995. Painting a new face on relationships: Relationship remodeling in response to chronic illness. In *Confronting Relationship Challenges*, eds. S. Duck and J. T. Wood, 181-210. Thousand Oaks, CA: Sage.

McNeill, J. J. 1988. *The Church and the Homosexual*. Boston: Beacon Press.

McWhirter, D. P., and A. M. Mattison. 1984. *The Male Couple: How Relationships Develop*. Englewood Cliffs: Prentice-Hall.

Manning, T. 1995. Assimilationism: Are you guilty or not guilty. *Gay Times* April: 19-24.

Marcus, E. 1988. *The Male Couple's Guide to Living Together*. New York: Harper & Row.

Meyer, J. 1990. Guess who's coming to dinner this time? A study of gay intimate relationships and the support for these relationships. *Marriage and Family Review* 14 (3/4): 59-82.

Modrcin, M. J., and N. L. Wyers. 1990. Lesbian and gay couples: Where they turn when help is needed. *Journal of Gay and Lesbian Psychotherapy* 1 (3): 89-104.

Monette, P. 1994. *Becoming a Man: Half a Life Story*. London: Abacus.

Morin, S. F. 1977. Heterosexual bias in psychological research on lesbianism and male homosexuality. *American Psychologist* 32 (8): 629-637.

Nanda, S., and J. S. Francher. 1980. Culture and homosexuality: A comparison of long term gay male and lesbian relationships. *The Eastern Anthropologist* 33: 139-152.

Parkin, F. 1968. *Middle Class Radicalism: The Social Bases of the British Campaign for Nuclear Disarmament*. Manchester: Manchester University Press.

Peck, S. 1993. *Further Along the Road Less Traveled: The Unending Journey towards Spiritual Growth*. London: Simon & Schuster.

Peplau, L. A. 1981. What homosexuals want in relationships. *Psychology Today* 15 (March): 28-38.

Peplau, L. A. 1982. Research on homosexual couples: An overview. *Journal of Homosexuality* 8 (2): 3-8.

Peplau, L. A., and S. D. Cochran. 1981. Value orientations in the intimate relationships of gay men. *Journal of Homosexuality* 6 (3): 1-19.

Peplau, L. A., and S. L. Gordon. 1983. The intimate relationships of lesbians and gay men. In *Changing Boundaries: Gender Roles and Sexual Behavior*, eds. E. R. Allgeier and N. B. McCormick, 226-244. Palo Alto, CA: Mayfield.

Plummer, K. 1975. *Sexual Stigma: An Interactionist Account*. London: Routledge & Kegan Paul.

Risman, B., and P. Schwartz. 1988. Sociological research on male and female homosexuality. *Annual Review of Sociology* 14: 125-147.

Rusbult, C. E. 1987. Responses to dissatisfaction in close relationships: The exit-voice-loyalty-neglect model. In *Intimate Relationships: Development, Dynamics, Deterioration*, eds. D. Perlman and S. W. Duck, 209-237. London: Sage.

Saghir, M., and E. Robins. 1973. *Male and Female Homosexuality: A Comprehensive Investigation*. Baltimore: Williams and Wilkins.

Sanderson, T. 1990. *Making Gay Relationships Work: A Handbook for Male Couples*. London: The Other Way Press.

Seow, C. L. 1996. *Homosexuality and Christian Community*. Louisville, Ky: Westminster John Knox Press.

Sherman, S. ed. 1996. *Lesbian and Gay Marriage*. Philadelphia: Temple University Press.

Silverstein, C. 1981. *Man To Man: Gay Couples in America*. New York: William Morrow.

Stuart, E., and A. Thatcher. 1996. *Christian Perspectives on Sexuality and Gender*. Leominster, UK: Gracewing.

Sullivan, A. 1995. *Virtually Normal: An Argument about Homosexuality*. New York: Picador.

Tessina, T. 1989. *Gay Relationships for Men and Women*. Los Angeles: Jeremy R. Tarcher.

Thumma, S. 1991. Negotiating a religious identity: The case of the gay evangelical. *Sociological Analysis* 52(4): 333-347.

Troiden, R. R. 1979. Becoming homosexual: A model of gay identity acquisition. *Psychiatry: Journal for the Study of Interpersonal Processes* 42: 362-373.

Troiden, R. R. 1984. Self, self-concept, identity, and homosexual identity:
    Constructs in need of and differentiation. *Journal of Homosexuality*
    10 (3&4): 97-107.
Vasey, M. 1996. *Friends and Strangers: A New Exploration of
    Homosexuality and the Bible.* London: Hodder & Stoughton.
Wagner, G., J. Serafini, J. Rabkin, R. Remien and J. Williams. 1994.
    Integration of one's religion and homosexuality: A weapon against
    internalized homophobia? *Journal of Homosexuality* 26 (4): 91-110.
Weatherburn, P. 1992. *The Relationship Between the Sexual Behaviour of
    Homosexually Active Men and Their Age and Relationship Types.*
    London: Project SIGMA, Paper No. 28.
Weeks, J. 1995. *Invented Moralities.* Cambridge: Polity Press.
Weinberg, M. S., and C. J. Williams. 1974. *Male Homosexuals: Their
    Problems and Adaptations.* New York: Penguin.
Wolfson, E. 1996. Why we should fight for the freedom to marry: The
    challenges and opportunities that will follow a win in Hawaii.
    *Journal of Gay, Lesbian and Bisexual Identity* 1 (1): 79-89.
Wood, J. T. 1994. Gender and relationship crises: Contrasting reasons,
    responses, and relational orientations. In *Queer Words, Queer
    Images: Communication of Homosexuality,* ed. R. J. Ringer, 238-264.
    New York: New York University Press.
Yip, A. K. T. 1991. *Social Censure of Homosexuality in the Protestant
    Church in England.* Unpublished M.Phil. Thesis, University of
    Cambridge, UK.
Yip, A. K. T. 1995a. *Gay Christian Partnerships.* Unpublished PhD Thesis,
    University of Surrey, Guildford, UK.
Yip, A. K. T. 1995b. Gay does not mean ungodly. *The Sunday Times,* 20
    August.
Yip, A. K. T. 1996a. Gay Christian couples and blessing ceremonies.
    *Theology and Sexuality* 4: 100-107.
Yip, A. K. T. 1996b. Gay Christians and their participation in the gay
    subculture. *Deviant Behavior* 17 (3): 297-318.
Yip, A. K. T. 1996c. Quest membership survey report. *Quest Chronicle*
    5&6: 2-23.
Yip, A. K. T. 1996d. Quest membership survey report [edited version]. *The
    Month: A Review of Christian Thought and World Affairs* 29 (11): 439-
    445.
Yip, A. K. T. 1997a. Attacking the attacker: Gay Christians talk back.
    *British Journal of Sociology* 48 (1): 113-127.
Yip, A. K. T. 1997b. Gay male Christian couples and sexual
    exclusivity. *Sociology* 31 (2): 1-18.
Yip, A. K. T. 1997c. Dare to differ: Gay and lesbian Catholics'
    assessment of official Catholic positions on sexuality. *Sociology of
    Religion* 58 (2): 165-180.
Yip, A. K. T. (Forthcoming). Gay Christians and their perceptions of the
    Christian community in relation to their sexuality. *Theology and
    Sexuality.*
Yip, A. K. T. (Forthcoming). The politics of counter-rejection: Gay
    Christians and the church. *Journal of Homosexuality.*

# Index

## About the Author

ANDREW K. T. YIP teaches sociology at the Nottingham Trent University in Britain where he is also the Deputy Director of the Crime and Social Research Unit (CSRU). He is currently undertaking a national survey of gay, lesbian, and bisexual Christians, and writing a book on the management of sexuality and spirituality among gay Christians. He also contributes actively to the work of the Centre for the Study of Christianity and Sexuality (CSCS).

ISBN 0-275-95730-6

90000>

9 780275 957308

EAN

HARDCOVER BAR CODE